5th Grade

CALIFORNIA

MATH TEST PREP

Common Core State Standards

INTRODUCTION

Our 5th Grade Math Test Prep for Common Core State Standards is an excellent resource to supplement your classroom's curriculum to assess and manage students' understanding of concepts outlined in the Common Core State Standards Initiative. This resource is divided into three sections: Diagnostic, Practice, and Assessment with multiple choice questions in each section. We recommend you use the Diagnostic section as a tool to determine the students' areas that need to be retaught. We also recommend you encourage your students to show their work to determine _how_ and _why_ the student arrived at an answer. The Practice section should be used to strengthen the students' knowledge by re-testing the standard to ensure comprehension of each standard. To ensure students' apply taught concepts in the classroom, we advise you use the Assessment section as a final test to verify the students' have mastered the standard.

This resource contains 600 practice problems aligned to the Common Core State Standards. To view the standards, refer to pages _i_ through _v_.

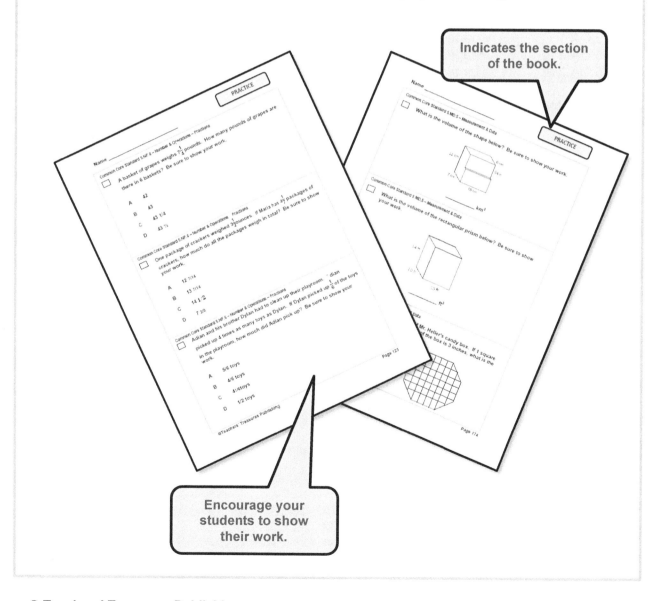

Indicates the section of the book.

Encourage your students to show their work.

5th Grade
Math Test Prep

FOR

Common Core
Standards

Operations & Algebraic Thinking   5.OA.1

Use parentheses, brackets, or braces in numerical expressions, and evaluate expressions with these symbols.

Operations & Algebraic Thinking   5.OA.2

Write simple expressions that record calculations with numbers, and interpret numerical expressions without evaluating them. *For example, express the calculation "add 8 and 7, then multiply by 2" as 2 × (8 + 7). Recognize that 3 × (18932 + 921) is three times as large as 18932 + 921, without having to calculate the indicated sum or product.*

Operations & Algebraic Thinking   5.OA.3

Generate two numerical patterns using two given rules. Identify apparent relationships between corresponding terms. Form ordered pairs consisting of corresponding terms from the two patterns, and graph the ordered pairs on a coordinate plane. *For example, given the rule "Add 3" and the starting number 0, and given the rule "Add 6" and the starting number 0, generate terms in the resulting sequences, and observe that the terms in one sequence are twice the corresponding terms in the other sequence. Explain informally why this is so.*

Number & Operations in Base Ten   5.NBT.1

Recognize that in a multi-digit number, a digit in one place represents 10 times as much as it represents in the place to its right and 1/10 of what it represents in the place to its left.

Number & Operations in Base Ten   5.NBT.2

Explain patterns in the number of zeros of the product when multiplying a number by powers of 10, and explain patterns in the placement of the decimal point when a decimal is multiplied or divided by a power of 10. Use whole-number exponents to denote powers of 10.

Number & Operations in Base Ten   5.NBT.3

Read, write, and compare decimals to thousandths. Read and write decimals to thousandths using base-ten numerals, number names, and expanded form, e.g., 347.392 = 3 × 100 + 4 × 10 + 7 × 1 + 3 × (1/10) + 9 × (1/100) + 2 × (1/1000). Compare two decimals to thousandths based on meanings of the digits in each place, using >, =, and < symbols to record the results of comparisons.

Number & Operations in Base Ten   **5.NBT.4**

Use place value understanding to round decimals to any place.

Number & Operations in Base Ten   **5.NBT.5**

Fluently multiply multi-digit whole numbers using the standard algorithm.

Number & Operations in Base Ten   **5.NBT.6**

Find whole-number quotients of whole numbers with up to four-digit dividends and two-digit divisors, using strategies based on place value, the properties of operations, and/or the relationship between multiplication and division. Illustrate and explain the calculation by using equations, rectangular arrays, and/or area models.

Number & Operations in Base Ten   **5.NBT.7**

Add, subtract, multiply, and divide decimals to hundredths, using concrete models or drawings and strategies based on place value, properties of operations, and/or the relationship between addition and subtraction; relate the strategy to a written method and explain the reasoning used.

Number & Operations - Fractions   **5.NF.1**

Add and subtract fractions with unlike denominators (including mixed numbers) by replacing given fractions with equivalent fractions in such a way as to produce an equivalent sum or difference of fractions with like denominators. *For example, 2/3 + 5/4 = 8/12 + 15/12 = 23/12. (In general, a/b + c/d = (ad + bc)/bd.)*

Number & Operations - Fractions   **5.NF.2**

Solve word problems involving addition and subtraction of fractions referring to the same whole, including cases of unlike denominators, e.g., by using visual fraction models or equations to represent the problem. Use benchmark fractions and number sense of fractions to estimate mentally and assess the reasonableness of answers. *For example, recognize an incorrect result 2/5 + 1/2 = 3/7, by observing that 3/7 < 1/2.*

Number & Operations - Fractions   **5.NF.3**

Interpret a fraction as division of the numerator by the denominator (*a*/*b* = *a* ÷ *b*). Solve word problems involving division of whole numbers leading to answers in the form of fractions or mixed numbers, e.g., by using visual fraction models or equations to represent the problem. *For example, interpret 3/4 as the result of dividing 3 by 4, noting that 3/4 multiplied by 4 equals 3, and that when 3 wholes are shared equally among 4 people each person has a share of size 3/4. If 9 people want to share a 50-pound sack of rice equally by weight, how many pounds of rice should each person get? Between what two whole numbers does your answer lie?*

Number & Operations - Fractions   **5.NF.4**

Apply and extend previous understandings of multiplication to multiply a fraction or whole number by a fraction. Interpret the product (*a*/*b*) × *q* as a parts of a partition of *q* into *b* equal parts; equivalently, as the result of a sequence of operations *a* × *q* ÷ *b*. *For example, use a visual fraction model to show (2/3) × 4 = 8/3, and create a story context for this equation. Do the same with (2/3) × (4/5) = 8/15. (In general, (a/b) × (c/d) = ac/bd.)* Find the area of a rectangle with fractional side lengths by tiling it with unit squares of the appropriate unit fraction side lengths, and show that the area is the same as would be found by multiplying the side lengths. Multiply fractional side lengths to find areas of rectangles, and represent fraction products as rectangular areas.

Number & Operations - Fractions   **5.NF.5**

Interpret multiplication as scaling (resizing), by:
> Comparing the size of a product to the size of one factor on the basis of the size of the other factor, without performing the indicated multiplication.
> Explaining why multiplying a given number by a fraction greater than 1 results in a product greater than the given number (recognizing multiplication by whole numbers greater than 1 as a familiar case); explaining why multiplying a given number by a fraction less than 1 results in a product smaller than the given number; and relating the principle of fraction equivalence *a*/*b* = (*n* × *a*)/(*n* × *b*) to the effect of multiplying *a*/*b* by 1.

Number & Operations - Fractions   **5.NF.6**

Solve real world problems involving multiplication of fractions and mixed numbers, e.g., by using visual fraction models or equations to represent the problem.

Number & Operations - Fractions   **5.NF.7**

Apply and extend previous understandings of division to divide unit fractions by whole numbers and whole numbers by unit fractions. Interpret division of a unit fraction by a non-zero whole number, and compute such quotients. *For example, create a story context for (1/3) ÷ 4, and use a visual fraction model to show the quotient. Use the relationship between multiplication and division to explain that (1/3) ÷ 4 = 1/12 because (1/12) × 4 = 1/3.* Interpret division of a whole number by a unit fraction, and compute such quotients. *For example, create a story context for 4 ÷ (1/5), and use a visual fraction model to show the quotient. Use the relationship between multiplication and division to explain that 4 ÷ (1/5) = 20 because 20 × (1/5) = 4.* Solve real world problems involving division of unit fractions by non-zero whole numbers and division of whole numbers by unit fractions, e.g., by using visual fraction models and equations to represent the problem. *For example, how much chocolate will each person get if 3 people share 1/2 lb of chocolate equally? How many 1/3-cup servings are in 2 cups of raisins?*

Measurement & Data   **5.MD.1**

Convert among different-sized standard measurement units within a given measurement system (e.g., convert 5 cm to 0.05 m), and use these conversions in solving multi-step, real world problems.

Measurement & Data   **5.MD.2**

Make a line plot to display a data set of measurements in fractions of a unit (1/2, 1/4, 1/8). Use operations on fractions for this grade to solve problems involving information presented in line plots. *For example, given different measurements of liquid in identical beakers, find the amount of liquid each beaker would contain if the total amount in all the beakers were redistributed equally.*

Measurement & Data   **5.MD.3**

Recognize volume as an attribute of solid figures and understand concepts of volume measurement. A cube with side length 1 unit, called a "unit cube," is said to have "one cubic unit" of volume, and can be used to measure volume. A solid figure which can be packed without gaps or overlaps using *n* unit cubes is said to have a volume of *n* cubic units.

Measurement & Data   **5.MD.4**

Measure volumes by counting unit cubes, using cubic cm, cubic in, cubic ft, and improvised units.

Measurement & Data 5.MD.5

Relate volume to the operations of multiplication and addition and solve real world and mathematical problems involving volume. Find the volume of a right rectangular prism with whole-number side lengths by packing it with unit cubes, and show that the volume is the same as would be found by multiplying the edge lengths, equivalently by multiplying the height by the area of the base. Represent threefold whole-number products as volumes, e.g., to represent the associative property of multiplication. Apply the formulas $V = l \times w \times h$ and $V = b \times h$ for rectangular prisms to find volumes of right rectangular prisms with whole-number edge lengths in the context of solving real world and mathematical problems. Recognize volume as additive. Find volumes of solid figures composed of two non-overlapping right rectangular prisms by adding the volumes of the non-overlapping parts, applying this technique to solve real world problems.

Geometry 5.G.1

Use a pair of perpendicular number lines, called axes, to define a coordinate system, with the intersection of the lines (the origin) arranged to coincide with the 0 on each line and a given point in the plane located by using an ordered pair of numbers, called its coordinates. Understand that the first number indicates how far to travel from the origin in the direction of one axis, and the second number indicates how far to travel in the direction of the second axis, with the convention that the names of the two axes and the coordinates correspond (e.g., x-axis and x-coordinate, y-axis and y-coordinate).

Geometry 5.G.2

Represent real world and mathematical problems by graphing points in the first quadrant of the coordinate plane, and interpret coordinate values of points in the context of the situation.

Geometry 5.G.3

Understand that attributes belonging to a category of two-dimensional figures also belong to all subcategories of that category. For example, all rectangles have four right angles and squares are rectangles, so all squares have four right angles.

Geometry 5.G.4

Classify two-dimensional figures in a hierarchy based on properties.

LENGTH

Metric	Customary
1 kilometer = 1000 meters	1 mile = 1760 yards
1 meter = 100 centimeters	1 mile = 5280 feet
1 centimeter = 10 millimeters	1 yard = 3 feet
	1 foot = 12 inches

CAPACITY & VOLUME

Metric	Customary
1 liter = 1000 milliliters	1 gallon = 4 quarts
	1 gallon = 128 ounces
	1 quart = 2 pints
	1 pint = 2 cups
	1 cup = 8 ounces

MASS & WEIGHT

Metric	Customary
1 kilogram = 1000 grams	1 ton = 2000 pounds
1 gram = 1000 milligrams	1 pound = 16 ounces

PERIMETER

square $P = 4s$

rectangle $P = 2l + 2w$ or $P = 2(l + w)$

AREA

square $\qquad A = s^2$

retangle $\qquad A = lw \qquad$ or $\qquad A = bh$

triangle $\qquad A = \dfrac{1}{2}bh \qquad$ or $\qquad A = \dfrac{bh}{2}$

TIME

1 year = 365 days

1 year = 12 months

1 year = 52 weeks

1 week = 7 days

1 day = 24 hours

1 hour = 60 minutes

1 minute = 60 seconds

Common Core Standard 5.OA.1 – Operations & Algebraic Thinking

☐ **Solve the numerical expression problem below. Be sure to show your work.**

$$(5 - 3)^2 \times 8 + 5^2 = \boxed{}$$

Common Core Standard 5.OA.1– Operations & Algebraic Thinking

☐ **Solve the numerical expression problem below. Be sure to show your work.**

$$36 + [8 + (7 \times 2)^2] - 4 = \boxed{}$$

Common Core Standard 5.OA.1 – Operations & Algebraic Thinking

☐ **Solve the numerical expression problem below. Be sure to show your work.**

$$(24 \div 6)^2 + (15 + 7) + 4^2 = \boxed{}$$

Common Core Standard 5.OA.1 – Operations & Algebraic Thinking

☐ **Solve the numerical expression problem below. Be sure to show your work.**

$$[\,(\,17 + 9\,) + (\,20 \div 2\,)^2\,] \times 5 = \boxed{}$$

Common Core Standard 5.OA.1 – Operations & Algebraic Thinking

☐ **Solve the numerical expression problem below. Be sure to show your work.**

$$(\,15 \div 3\,)^2 + [\,(\,18 + 2\,)^2 + 9\,] = \boxed{}$$

Common Core Standard 5.OA.1 – Operations & Algebraic Thinking

☐ **Solve the numerical expression problem below. Be sure to show your work.**

$$(\,9 + 6\,)^2 \times 3^2 \div 25 = \boxed{}$$

Common Core Standard 5.OA.1 – Operations & Algebraic Thinking

☐ **Solve the numerical expression problem below. Be sure to show your work.**

$$(36 \div 12) + (9 \div 3)^2 - 5 = \boxed{}$$

Common Core Standard 5.OA.1– Operations & Algebraic Thinking

☐ **Solve the numerical expression problem below. Be sure to show your work.**

$$[(12 - 9) + (12 \div 6)^2] \times 6 = \boxed{}$$

Common Core Standard 5.OA.1 – Operations & Algebraic Thinking

☐ **Solve the numerical expression problem below. Be sure to show your work.**

$$22 + 13 \times (12 + 5) + 3^2 = \boxed{}$$

Common Core Standard 5.OA.1 – Operations & Algebraic Thinking

☐ **Solve the numerical expression problem below. Be sure to show your work.**

$$(27 \div 9) + (45 \div 9)^2 - 10 = \boxed{}$$

Common Core Standard 5.OA.1– Operations & Algebraic Thinking

☐ **Solve the numerical expression problem below. Be sure to show your work.**

$$63 + (36 \div 4)^2 + (10 - 2) = \boxed{}$$

Common Core Standard 5.OA.1 – Operations & Algebraic Thinking

☐ **Solve the numerical expression problem below. Be sure to show your work.**

$$38 + 11 \times (9 + 3) + 6^2 = \boxed{}$$

Common Core Standard 5.OA.1 – Operations & Algebraic Thinking

☐ **Solve the numerical expression problem below. Be sure to show your work.**

$$(\ 3 \times 4 \ )^2 \times 10 + 5^2 = \boxed{}$$

Common Core Standard 5.OA.1 – Operations & Algebraic Thinking

☐ **Solve the numerical expression problem below. Be sure to show your work.**

$$8^2 - (\ 20 \div 10 \ ) + (\ 9^2 \div 3 \ ) = \boxed{}$$

Common Core Standard 5.OA.1 – Operations & Algebraic Thinking

☐ **Solve the numerical expression problem below. Be sure to show your work.**

$$(\ 56 \div 8 \ )^2 \div (\ 16 - 9 \ ) \times 6^2 = \boxed{}$$

Common Core Standard 5.OA.1 – Operations & Algebraic Thinking

☐ **Solve the numerical expression problem below. Be sure to show your work.**

$$[(12 + 9)^2 + 39] \div 12 = \boxed{}$$

Common Core Standard 5.OA.1– Operations & Algebraic Thinking

☐ **Solve the numerical expression problem below. Be sure to show your work.**

$$65 - [(5 \times 9) + (10^2 \div 25)] = \boxed{}$$

Common Core Standard 5.OA.1 – Operations & Algebraic Thinking

☐ **Solve the numerical expression problem below. Be sure to show your work.**

$$[(16 - 3)^2 + (3 \times 6)^2] \times 3^2 = \boxed{}$$

Common Core Standard 5.OA.1 – Operations & Algebraic Thinking

☐ **Solve the numerical expression problem below. Be sure to show your work.**

$$98 - [\,(\,25 \div 5\,)^2 - 18\,] \times 12 = \boxed{}$$

Common Core Standard 5.OA.1– Operations & Algebraic Thinking

☐ **Solve the numerical expression problem below. Be sure to show your work.**

$$14^2 + (\,60 \div 30 + 2^2\,) + 4 = \boxed{}$$

Common Core Standard 5.OA.1 – Operations & Algebraic Thinking

☐ **Solve the numerical expression problem below. Be sure to show your work.**

$$(\,70 \div 35\,)^2 + (\,10 + 4\,) \times 6^2 = \boxed{}$$

Common Core Standard 5.OA.1 – Operations & Algebraic Thinking

☐ **Solve the numerical expression problem below. Be sure to show your work.**

$$[(11 - 6)^2 + 13] \times (5^2 - 18) = \boxed{}$$

Common Core Standard 5.OA.1– Operations & Algebraic Thinking

☐ **Solve the numerical expression problem below. Be sure to show your work.**

$$[15^2 - (32 \div 8 - 2^2)] + 4 = \boxed{}$$

Common Core Standard 5.OA.1 – Operations & Algebraic Thinking

☐ **Solve the numerical expression problem below. Be sure to show your work.**

$$[(49 \div 7)^2 + 6^2] \div (5 \times 1) = \boxed{}$$

Common Core Standard 5.OA.2 – Operations & Algebraic Thinking

☐ **Find the correct numerical expression that matches the simple expression below:**

> *Fifteen more than the quotient of fifty-four divided by nine.*

A $(15 + 9) \div 54$

B $54 \div 9 + 15$

C $15 (54 \div 9)$

D $(54 + 15) / 9$

Common Core Standard5.OA.2– Operations & Algebraic Thinking

☐ **Find the correct simple expression that matches the numerical expression below:**

> *25 x (20 – 15)*

A   Twenty-five times the difference of twenty and fifteen.

B   Twenty-five more than the difference of twenty and fifteen.

C   Fifteen less than twenty-five times twenty

D   Twenty times the difference of twenty-five and fifteen.

Common Core Standard 5.OA.2 – Operations & Algebraic Thinking

☐ **Find the correct numerical expression that matches the simple expression below:**

> *Forty-six times the difference of fifty-eight and fifty-six.*

A $(46 - 58) \times 56$

B $(56 - 58) \times 46$

C $46 \times (58 - 56)$

D $46 + (58 - 56)$

Common Core Standard 5.OA.2 – Operations & Algebraic Thinking

☐ **Find the correct simple expression that matches the numerical expression:**

$$3 \times (12 - 4)$$

A Four less than the product of three and twelve.

B Three times than the difference of twelve and four.

C Quotient of three and the difference of twelve and four.

D Four less than the quotient of twelve and four.

Common Core Standard 5.OA.2 – Operations & Algebraic Thinking

☐ **Find the correct numerical expression that matches the simple expression:**

Ten less than the addition of thirty-three and twenty-seven.

A 33 + 27 – 10

B 10 (33 + 27)

C (32 + 27) – 10

D 10 – 33 + 27

Common Core Standard 5.OA.2 – Operations & Algebraic Thinking

☐ **Find the correct simple expression that matches the numerical expression below:**

$$48 \div 12 - 4$$

A Twelve less than four divided by the quotient of forty-eight.

B Four less than the quotient of forty-eight divided by twelve.

C Quotient of forty-eight less than twelve and four.

D Four less than forty-eight times twelve.

Common Core Standard 5.OA.2 – Operations & Algebraic Thinking

☐ **Find the correct simple expression that matches the numerical expression below:**

$$27 \times (57 + 19)$$

A Twenty-seven more than the addition of fifty-seven and nineteen.

B Nineteen more than twenty-seven times fifty-seven.

C Twenty-seven times the addition of fifty-seven and nineteen.

D Twenty-seven more than the addition of fifty-seven and nineteen.

Common Core Standard 5.OA.2 – Operations & Algebraic Thinking

☐ **Find the correct numerical expression that matches the simple expression:**

Ten greater than the addition of thirty-three and twenty-seven.

A $33 + 27 + 10$

B $10 (33 + 27)$

C $33 + (27 - 10)$

D $10 - 33 + 27$

Common Core Standard 5.OA.2 – Operations & Algebraic Thinking

☐ **Find the correct simple expression that matches the numerical expression below:**

$$144 \div 12 + 15$$

A Fifteen more than the quotient of one hundred forty-four divided by twelve.

B Fifteen times the quotient of one hundred forty-four divided by twelve.

C The addition of twelve and fifteen divided by one hundred forty-four.

D One hundred forty-four divided by the addition of twelve and fifteen.

Common Core Standard 5.OA.2 – Operations & Algebraic Thinking

☐ **Find the correct numerical expression that matches the simple expression:**

> *Four less than the quotient of forty divided by two.*

A $4 - 40 \div 2$

B $40 \times 2 - 4$

C $40 \div 2 - 4$

D $40 \div (2 - 4)$

Common Core Standard 5.OA.2 – Operations & Algebraic Thinking

☐ **Find the correct simple expression that matches the numerical expression below:**

> $32 \times (32 - 18)$

A   Thirty-two more than the difference of thirty-two and eighteen.

B   Thirty-two times the difference of thirty-two and eighteen.

C   The difference of thirty-two and eighteen more than thirty-two.

D   Thirty-two times thirty-two less than eighteen.

Common Core Standard 5.OA.2 – Operations & Algebraic Thinking

☐ **Find the correct numerical expression that matches the simple expression:**

> *Six times the addition of thirteen and five.*

A $6 \times 5 + 13$

B $6 \times 13 + 5$

C $6 \times (13 + 5)$

D $6 + (13 + 5)$

Common Core Standard 5.OA.2 – Operations & Algebraic Thinking

Find the correct simple expression that matches the numerical expression below:

$$35 \div 16 - 9$$

A   Nine more than the quotient of thirty-five divided by sixteen.

B   Thirty-five divided by nine less sixteen.

C   Sixteen less nine divided by the quotient of thirty-five.

D   Nine less than the quotient of thirty-five divided by sixteen.

Common Core Standard 5.OA.2 – Operations & Algebraic Thinking

Find the correct numerical expression that matches the simple expression:

Thirty-six times the addition of twenty-two and thirty-one.

A   (36 x 22) + 31

B   36 x (22+ 31)

C   36 + (22 +31)

D   36 + (22 x 31)

Common Core Standard 5.OA.2 – Operations & Algebraic Thinking

Find the correct simple expression that matches the numerical expression below:

$$97 + 34 - 18$$

A   Eighteen more than the addition of ninety-seven and thirty-four.

B   Ninety-seven subtracted from thirty-four minus eighteen.

C   Eighteen less than the addition of ninety-seven and thirty-four.

D   Ninety-seven less than the difference of thirty-four and eighteen.

Common Core Standard 5.OA.2 – Operations & Algebraic Thinking

☐ **Find the correct numerical expression below that matches the simple expression:**

> *Seventy-five times the difference of forty and thirty-five.*

A   75 x 40 - 35

B   75 x (40 – 35)

C   75 + 40 - 35

D   (75 x 40) – 35

Common Core Standard 5.OA.2 – Operations & Algebraic Thinking

☐ **Find the correct simple expression that matches the numerical expression below:**

> *47 x (71 – 19)*

A   Forty-seven more than the difference of seventy-one and nineteen.

B   Forty-seven times the difference of seventy-one and nineteen.

C   The difference of seventy-one and nineteen times forty-seven.

D   Forty-seven times seventy-one less than nineteen.

Common Core Standard 5.OA.2 – Operations & Algebraic Thinking

☐ **Find the correct numerical expression below that matches the simple expression:**

> *Six less than the addition of sixty-two and forty-seven.*

A   6 – 62 + 47

B   62 + 47 – 6

C   62 + (47 + 6)

D   62 x 47 - 6

Name _____

Common Core Standard 5.OA.2 – Operations & Algebraic Thinking

☐   **Find the correct simple expression that matches the numerical expression below:**

$$88+ 19 -12$$

A   Twelve less than the addition of eighty-eight and nineteen.

B   Eight-eight times the difference of nineteen and twelve.

C   Eighty-eight less than the difference of nineteen and twelve.

D   Twelve less than the multiplication of eighty-eight and nineteen.

Common Core Standard 5.OA.2 – Operations & Algebraic Thinking

☐   **Find the correct numerical expression that matches the simple expression:**

Forty-two times the addition of forty-four and twelve.

A   44 + 12 x 42

B   42 x 44 + 12

C   42 x (44 + 12)

D   42 + (44 + 12)

Common Core Standard 5.OA.2 – Operations & Algebraic Thinking

☐   **Find the correct simple numerical expression that matches the equation below:**

$$69 \div 12 - 9$$

A   Twelve less than nine divided by the quotient of sixty-nine.

B   Nine more than the quotient of sixty-nine and twelve.

C   Nine less than the quotient of sixty-nine and twelve.

D   Sixty-nine divided by twelve less than nine.

Common Core Standard 5.OA.2 – Operations & Algebraic Thinking

[ ]   **Find the correct numerical expression below that matches the simple expression:**

> *Eight less than the quotient of seventy-three divided by twenty-four.*

A $73 \div (24 - 8)$

B $73 \div 24 - 8$

C $8 - 73 \div 24$

D $8 - (73 \div 24)$

Common Core Standard 5.OA.2 – Operations & Algebraic Thinking

[ ]   **Find the correct simple expression that matches the numerical expression below:**

> $27 \times (18 - 12)$

A   Twenty-seven times the difference of eighteen and twelve.

B   Eighteen less than twelve divided by the quotient of twenty-seven.

C   Twenty-seven more the difference of eighteen and twelve.

D   Twenty-seven times eighteen less than twelve.

Common Core Standard 5.OA.2 – Operations & Algebraic Thinking

[ ]   **Find the correct numerical expression below that matches the simple expression:**

> *Seven less than the quotient of twelve divided by five.*

A $7 - (12 \div 5)$

B $12 \div (5 - 7)$

C $(5 - 7) \div 12$

D $12 \div 5 - 7$

Name _____

Common Core Standard 5.OA.3 – Operations & Algebraic Thinking

Use table to answer the questions below

x	0	1	2	3
y	0	3	6	9

☐ **Which rule below best fits the data in the table?**

A   y = x + 3

B   y = x/3

C   y = 3x

D   x = 3y

Common Core Standard5.OA.3 – Operations & Algebraic Thinking

☐ **Which rule below best fits the data in row x?**

A   add 1

B   add 2

C   add 3

D   add 4

Common Core Standard 5.OA.3 – Operations & Algebraic Thinking

☐ **Which rule below best fits the data in row y?**

A   add 1

B   add 2

C   add 3

D   add 4

Common Core Standard 5.OA.3 – Operations & Algebraic Thinking

Use table to answer the questions below

a	0	2	4	6
b	3	5	7	9

☐ **Which rule below best fits the data in the table?**

A   b = a + 2

B   b = a + 3

C   b = 3a

D   b = 3b

Common Core Standard5.OA.3 – Operations & Algebraic Thinking

☐ **Which rule below best fits the data in row _a_?**

A   add 1

B   add 2

C   add 3

D   add 4

Common Core Standard 5.OA.3 – Operations & Algebraic Thinking

☐ **Which rule below best fits the data in row _b_?**

A   multiply by 2

B   subtract 1

C   add 2

D   divide by 3

Name _____

Common Core Standard 5.OA.3 – Operations & Algebraic Thinking

Use table to answer the questions below

g	1	2	4	8
h	3	6	12	24

☐   **Which rule below best fits the data in the table?**

A   h = g + 2

B   h = g + 3

C   h = 3g

D   h = 3h

Common Core Standard5.OA.3 – Operations & Algebraic Thinking

☐   **Which rule below best fits the data in row *g*?**

A   multiply by 2

B   add 2

C   multiply by 3

D   add 4

Common Core Standard 5.OA.3 – Operations & Algebraic Thinking

☐   **Which rule below best fits the data in row *h*?**

A   subtract 3

B   multiply by 2

C   add 2

D   divide by 3

Name _____

Common Core Standard 5.OA.3 – Operations & Algebraic Thinking

Use table to answer the questions below

s	4	3	2	1
t	2	1.5	1	0.5

☐   **Which rule below best fits the data in the table?**

A   s = t + 2

B   t = s + 2

C   s = 2t

D   t = 2s

Common Core Standard5.OA.3 – Operations & Algebraic Thinking

☐   **Which rule below best fits the data in row _s_?**

A   add 1

B   subtract 1

C   add 0.5

D   subtract 0.5

Common Core Standard 5.OA.3 – Operations & Algebraic Thinking

☐   **Which rule below best fits the data in row _t_?**

A   subtract 1

B   add 1

C   subtract 0.5

D   add 0.5

Name _____

Common Core Standard 5.OA.3 – Operations & Algebraic Thinking

Use graph to answer the questions below

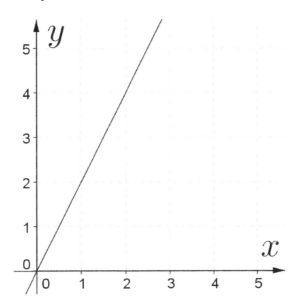

☐   **Which rule generates data in the graph?**

A $y = x + 1$ C $x = 2y$

B $y = x + 2$ D $y = 2x$

Common Core Standard5.OA.3 – Operations & Algebraic Thinking

☐   **Which rule generates data in the x-axis?**

A   add 2   C   multiply by 2

B   add 1   D   divide by 3

Common Core Standard 5.OA.3 – Operations & Algebraic Thinking

☐   **Which rule generates data in the y-axis?**

A   subtract 1   C   multiply by 2

B   add 2   D   divide by 1

Name _____

Common Core Standard 5.OA.3 – Operations & Algebraic Thinking

Use graph to answer the questions below

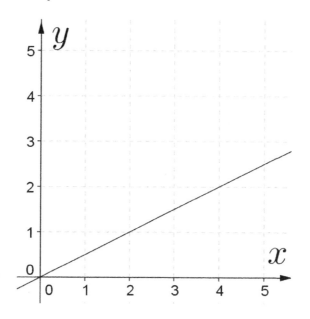

☐ **Which rule generates data in the graph?**

A $y = x + 1$ C $y = 2x$

B $y = x + 2$ D $x = 2y$

Common Core Standard5.OA.3 – Operations & Algebraic Thinking

☐ **Which rule generates data in the x-axis?**

A add 2   C add 1

B subtract 1   D divide by 1

Common Core Standard 5.OA.3 – Operations & Algebraic Thinking

☐ **Which rule generates data in the y-axis?**

A subtract 1   C multiply by 2

B add 1   D divide by 2

Name _____

Common Core Standard 5.OA.3 – Operations & Algebraic Thinking

Use table to answer the questions below

y	1	3	5	7
z	3	7	11	15

☐   **Which rule below best fits the data in the table?**

A $y = z + 2$

B $z = y + 2$

C $z = 2y + 1$

D $y = 2z + 1$

Common Core Standard5.OA.3 – Operations & Algebraic Thinking

☐   **Which rule below best fits the data in row y?**

A   subtract 2

B   multiply by 3

C   add 2

D   divide by 3

Common Core Standard 5.OA.3 – Operations & Algebraic Thinking

☐   **Which rule below best fits the data in row z?**

A   subtract 4

B   add 4

C   multiply by 4

D   divide by 4

Common Core Standard 5.OA.3 – Operations & Algebraic Thinking

Use graph to answer the questions below

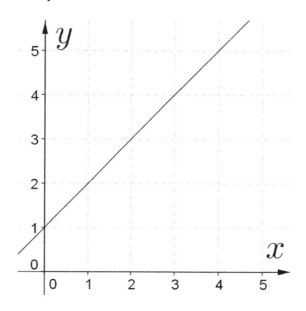

☐ **Which rule generates data in the graph?**

A $y = x + 1$ C $x = 2y$

B $y = x + 2$ D $y = 2x$

Common Core Standard5.OA.3 – Operations & Algebraic Thinking

☐ **Which rule generates data in the x-axis?**

A   subtract 2   C   add 2

B   subtract 1   D   add 1

Common Core Standard 5.OA.3 – Operations & Algebraic Thinking

☐ **Which rule generates data in the y-axis?**

A   subtract 1   C   add 1

B   multiply by 2   D   divide by 2

Common Core Standard 5.NBT.1 – Number & Operations in Base Ten

☐ **What is the correct answer for the problem below?**

1000 + 500 + 60 + 3 =

A   10563

B   1563

C   1000500603

D   105603

Common Core Standard 5.NBT.1 – Number & Operations in Base Ten

☐ **What is the place value for the underlined number below?**

563.76<u>9</u>

A   Hundredths' place

B   Thousandths' place

C   Tenths' place

D   Ones' place

Common Core Standard 5.NBT.1 – Number & Operations in Base Ten

☐ **What digit is in the hundredths' place of the number below?**

1468.375

A   7

B   5

C   3

D   4

Common Core Standard 5.NBT.1 – Number & Operations in Base Ten

☐ **What digit is in the thousandths' place of the number below?**

7397.154

A   5

B   1

C   4

D   7

Common Core Standard 5.NBT.1 – Number & Operations in Base Ten

☐ **What is the place value for the underlined number below?**

9836.1475

A   Tens place

B   Tenths' place

C   Hundredths' place

D   Thousands' place

Common Core Standard 5.NBT.1 – Number & Operations in Base Ten

☐ **What is the correct answer for the problem below?**

600 + 30 + 7 =

A   637

B   6037

C   6307

D   600307

Name _____

Common Core Standard 5.NBT.1 – Number & Operations in Base Ten

☐ **What digit is in the tens' place of the number below?**

8723.649

A   6

B   2

C   7

D   4

Common Core Standard 5.NBT.1 – Number & Operations in Base Ten

☐ **What is the place value for the underlined number below?**

387.3987
‾

A   Tens' place

B   Hundreds' place

C   Thousands' place

D   Hundredths' place

Common Core Standard 5.NBT.1 – Number & Operations in Base Ten

☐ **What is the correct answer for the problem below?**

9000 + 300 + 40 + 1 =

A   9000300401

B   90341

C   93401

D   9341

Common Core Standard 5.NBT.1 – Number & Operations in Base Ten

☐ **What is the correct answer for the problem below?**

$$50000 + 6000 + 200 + 90 + 6 =$$

A   562906

B   506296

C   500006000200906

D   56296

Common Core Standard 5.NBT.1 – Number & Operations in Base Ten

☐ **What is the place value for the underlined number below?**

1296.32<u>9</u>5

A   Hundredths' place

B   Tenths' place

C   Thousandths' place

D   Millionths' place

Common Core Standard 5.NBT.1 – Number & Operations in Base Ten

☐ **What digit is in the thousands' place of the number below?**

9173.825

A   9

B   5

C   1

D   2

Name _____

Common Core Standard 5.NBT.1 – Number & Operations in Base Ten

☐   **What is the correct answer for the problem below?**

10000 + 9000 + 700 + 40 + 9 =

A   109749

B   19749

C   100009000700409

D   197409

Common Core Standard 5.NBT.1 – Number & Operations in Base Ten

☐   **What is the place value for the underlined number below?**

9375.641<u>8</u>

A   Hundredths' place

B   Tenths' place

C   Thousandths' place

D   Ten thousandths' place

Common Core Standard 5.NBT.1 – Number & Operations in Base Ten

☐   **What digit is in the hundredths' place of the number below?**

7485.621

A   4

B   7

C   1

D   2

Name _____

Common Core Standard 5.NBT.1 – Number & Operations in Base Ten

[ ] **What digit is in the thousands' place of the number below?**

74528.169

A   6

B   9

C   7

D   4

Common Core Standard 5.NBT.1 – Number & Operations in Base Ten

[ ] **What is the place value for the underlined number below?**

567.14<u>8</u>3

A   Thousands' place

B   Hundreds' place

C   Thousandths' place

D   Hundredths' place

Common Core Standard 5.NBT.1 – Number & Operations in Base Ten

[ ] **What is the correct answer for the problem below?**

300 + 80 + 2 =

A   3802

B   3082

C   382

D   300802

Name _____

Common Core Standard 5.NBT.1 – Number & Operations in Base Ten

☐ **What digit is in the hundredths' place of the number below?**

541.982

A   5

B   8

C   2

D   4

Common Core Standard 5.NBT.1 – Number & Operations in Base Ten

☐ **What is the place value for the underlined number below?**

11<u>1</u>1.1111

A   Tens' place

B   Ones' place

C   Tenths' place

D   Hundreds' place

Common Core Standard 5.NBT.1 – Number & Operations in Base Ten

☐ **What is the correct answer for the problem below?**

9000 + 900 + 90 =

A   900090090

B   9999

C   99090

D   9990

Common Core Standard 5.NBT.1 – Number & Operations in Base Ten

☐ **What is the correct answer for the problem below?**

200000 + 80000 + 6000 + 400 =

A   200,000,800,006,000,400

B   286,400

C   286,040

D   28,640

Common Core Standard 5.NBT.1 – Number & Operations in Base Ten

☐ **What is the place value for the underlined number below?**

12587.998

A   Thousands' place

B   Hundredths' place

C   Thousandths' place

D   Hundreds' place

Common Core Standard 5.NBT.1 – Number & Operations in Base Ten

☐ **What digit is in the tenths' place of the number below?**

3574.8921

A   4

B   8

C   7

D   9

Common Core Standard 5.NBT.2 – Number & Operations in Base Ten

☐ Solve the multiplication problem below. Be sure to show your work.

$$6.2 \times 10^5 =$$

A 62,000

B 620,000

C 6,200,000

D 6,200

Common Core Standard 5.NBT.2 – Number & Operations in Base Ten

☐ Solve the multiplication problem below. Be sure to show your work.

$$.99 \times 10 =$$

A 99

B 990

C 9.9

D 9900

Common Core Standard 5.NBT.2 – Number & Operations in Base Ten

☐ Juan bought 10^3 baseball cards. If each card cost $.05, how much did Juan spend? Be sure to show your work.

A $5.00

B $50.00

C $500.00

D $.50

Common Core Standard 5.NBT.2 – Number & Operations in Base Ten

☐ **Find the correct missing value in the problem below. Be sure to show your work.**

$$\_\_\_\_ \times 9 = 27000$$

A 300

B 30,000

C 3,000

D 3,000,000

Common Core Standard 5.NBT.2 – Number & Operations in Base Ten

☐ **Solve the multiplication problem below. Be sure to show your work.**

$$53 \times 10^2 =$$

A 530

B 5,300

C 53,000

D 53

Common Core Standard 5.NBT.2 – Number & Operations in Base Ten

☐ **Solve the multiplication problem below. Be sure to show your work.**

$$7.258 \times 10 =$$

A .7258

B 7258

C 725.8

D 72.58

Common Core Standard 5.NBT.2 – Number & Operations in Base Ten

☐ Solve the multiplication problem below. Be sure to show your work.

$$.5247 \times 10^2 =$$

A   5247

B   524.7

C   5.247

D   52.47

Common Core Standard 5.NBT.2 – Number & Operations in Base Ten

☐ Solve the multiplication problem below. Be sure to show your work.

$$87.25 \times 100 =$$

A   872.5

B   8.725

C   8,725

D   87,250

Common Core Standard 5.NBT.2 – Number & Operations in Base Ten

☐ Kathy has 10^2 mini cupcakes for her class. How many mini cupcakes does she have in total? Be sure to show your work.

A   100

B   1000

C   10

D   10000

Common Core Standard 5.NBT.2 – Number & Operations in Base Ten

☐ **Find the correct missing value in the problem below. Be sure to show your work.**

$$3000 \div \underline{\quad} = 15$$

A   20

B   2000

C   200

D   2

Common Core Standard 5.NBT.2 – Number & Operations in Base Ten

☐ **Solve the multiplication problem below. Be sure to show your work.**

$$7.125 \times 10^4 =$$

A   712.5

B   7,125

C   71,250

D   71.25

Common Core Standard 5.NBT.2 – Number & Operations in Base Ten

☐ **Solve the divison problem below. Be sure to show your work.**

$$10^4 \div 500 =$$

A   200

B   2000

C   2

D   20

Name _____

Common Core Standard 5.NBT.2 – Number & Operations in Base Ten

☐ **Find the correct missing value in the problem below. Be sure to show your work.**

$$12000 \div \underline{\quad} = 30$$

A   4000

B   400

C   40

D   4

Common Core Standard 5.NBT.2 – Number & Operations in Base Ten

☐ **Solve the division problem below. Be sure to show your work.**

$$924.57 \div 10^3 =$$

A   9.2457

B   0.92457

C   92.457

D   924.57

Common Core Standard 5.NBT.2 – Number & Operations in Base Ten

☐ **Solve the problem below. Be sure to show your work.**

$$10^4 \times 18 =$$

A   1,800

B   18,000

C   180,000

D   1,800,000

Common Core Standard 5.NBT.2 – Number & Operations in Base Ten

☐   **Solve the multiplication problem below. Be sure to show your work.**

$$.0157 \times 10^4 =$$

A   157

B   15.7

C   1.57

D   1570

Common Core Standard 5.NBT.2 – Number & Operations in Base Ten

☐   **Solve the multiplication problem below. Be sure to show your work.**

$$9.999 \times 1000 =$$

A   99.99

B   999.9

C   9,999

D   99,990

Common Core Standard 5.NBT.2 – Number & Operations in Base Ten

☐   **Jude went to the annual Plano Balloon Festival where he saw 10^3 balloons. How many balloons did Jude see in total? Be sure to show your work.**

A   10,000

B   1,000

C   10

D   100

Common Core Standard 5.NBT.2 – Number & Operations in Base Ten

☐　　Solve the multiplication problem below. Be sure to show your work.

$$.0028 \times 10^5 =$$

A　　28

B　　280

C　　.028

D　　2800

Common Core Standard 5.NBT.2 – Number & Operations in Base Ten

☐　　Solve the multiplication problem below. Be sure to show your work.

$$19.945 \times 10 =$$

A　　1994.5

B　　19.945

C　　199.45

D　　1.9945

Common Core Standard 5.NBT.2 – Number & Operations in Base Ten

☐　　Carolina bought some candy for Halloween. She bought 10^3 pieces of candy. Each piece costs $.15. How much did Carolina pay in total for all the candy? Be sure to show your work.

A　　$15.00

B　　$1.50

C　　$1500.00

D　　$150.00

Common Core Standard 5.NBT.2 – Number & Operations in Base Ten

☐ **Find the correct missing value in the problem below. Be sure to show your work.**

$$63 \times \underline{\quad} = 18{,}900$$

A   300

B   30

C   3

D   3000

Common Core Standard 5.NBT.2 – Number & Operations in Base Ten

☐ **Solve the multiplication problem below. Be sure to show your work.**

$$6.8479 \times 10^5 =$$

A   684.79

B   6847.9

C   684,790

D   68.479

Common Core Standard 5.NBT.2 – Number & Operations in Base Ten

☐ **Solve the multiplication problem below. Be sure to show your work.**

$$10^3 \times 29 =$$

A   290,000

B   2,900

C   29,000

D   290

Common Core Standard 5.NBT.3 – Number & Operations in Base Ten

☐   Some fifth grade girls competed in a race during PE. Suzanne finished in thirty-four and twenty-seven hundredths seconds. How did the scorekeeper write her time?

    A   34 sec

    B   27 sec

    C   34.27 sec

    D   27.34 sec

Common Core Standard 5.NBT.3 – Number & Operations in Base Ten

☐   Hank Aaron's batting average was 0.328 in 1956. In 1957 it was 0.355. Which of the following statements is true?

    A $0.328 < 0.355$

    B $0.328 > 0.355$

    C $0.328 = 0.355$

    D $0.355 < 0.328$

Common Core Standard 5.NBT.3 – Number & Operations in Base Ten

☐   Which of the following is in order from the greatest to the least?

    A   0.603, 0.67, 0.613, 0.610

    B   0.67, 0.613, 0.610, 0.603

    C   0.610, 0.613, 0.603, 0.67

    D   0.603, 0.610, 0.613, 0.67

Common Core Standard 5.NBT.3 – Number & Operations in Base Ten

☐ Jesse Owens set a world record of 10.3 seconds in the 100 meter dash in the 1936 Olympics in Germany. Which of the following is the correct way to read that world record time?

A   One and three tenths seconds

B   Ten point three seconds

C   Ten and three tenths of a seconds

D   Ten seconds and 3 more

Common Core Standard 5.NBT.3 – Number & Operations in Base Ten

☐ Derek Jeter's batting averages are listed below. Using his averages, which of the following statements is true?

A   Derek Jeter's best year was 2008.

B   Derek Jeter's average in 2007 was better than his 2010 average.

C   Derek Jeter's 2010 average was better than his 2007 average, but less than his 2008 average.

D   Derek Jeter's lowest average was in 2010.

Year	Average
2007	.322
2008	.363
2009	.406
2010	.330

Common Core Standard 5.NBT.3 – Number & Operations in Base Ten

☐ The school nurse weighed Aaron and told him he weighed seventy-six and eight tenths pounds. How did she write his weight on his chart?

A   768 pounds

B   7.68 pounds

C   76.8 pounds

D   0.768 pounds

Common Core Standard 5.NBT.3 – Number & Operations in Base Ten

☐ During the family vacation Mr. Sutton kept a record of the amount of gasoline he bought at each station. At the first gas station he purchased twenty-one and three tenths gallons. Which of the following shows how he wrote the gallons of gasoline at his first station?

A   213 gal

B   21.03 gal

C   2.13 gal

D   21.3 gal

Common Core Standard 5.NBT.3 – Number & Operations in Base Ten

☐ A weather bureau recorded the amount of rainfall for several months. In March it rained 3.93 inches. In April the bureau recorded 4.75 inches, and in May 3.09 inches. In June the bureau reported 3.5 inches. How should these amounts be listed in order from the least to the greatest?

A   3.5 in,   3.09 in,   3.93 in,   4.75 in

B   3.09 in,   3.5 in,   3.93 in,   4.75 in

C   4.75 in,   3.93 in,   3.5 in,   3.09 in

D   3.09 in,   3.93 in,   3.5 in,   4.75 in

Common Core Standard 5.NBT.3 – Number & Operations in Base Ten

☐ There was a jar with 3.09 liters of punch left from the school party. Which of the following is the correct way to read that amount?

A   Three hundred nine

B   Three hundred nine thousandths

C   Three and nine tenths

D   Three and nine hundredths

Common Core Standard 5.NBT.3 – Number & Operations in Base Ten

☐ How should four hundred sixty-nine thousandths be written as a number?

A   0.469

B   4.69

C   46.9

D   469,000

Common Core Standard 5.NBT.3 – Number & Operations in Base Ten

☐ Edwin Moses won the 400 meter hurdles race in the 1976 Montreal Olympics with a time of 47.67 seconds. Which of the following is the correct way to read his winning time?

A   Forty-seven point six seven seconds

B   Forty-seven and sixty-seven hundredths seconds

C   Forty-seven sixty-seven seconds

D   Forty-seven and sixty-seven tenths seconds

Common Core Standard 5.NBT.3 – Number & Operations in Base Ten

☐ Some of the teachers in Juanita's school have started a balanced diet. As a result, Mrs. Blanche lost 5.8 pounds, Mr. Brown lost 4.68 pounds, Ms. Turner lost 5.33 pounds, while her best friend Ms. Jackson lost 4.06 pounds. How would you put the weight lossess in order from the least to the most weight loss?

A   4.66 lbs, 4.06 lbs, 5.33 lbs, 5.8 lbs

B   5.8 lbs, 5.33 lbs, 4.66 lbs, 4.06 lbs

C   4.06 lbs, 4.68 lbs, 5.33 lbs, 5.8 lbs

D   5.33 lbs, 4.06 lbs, 4.66 lbs, 5.8 lbs

Name _____

Common Core Standard 5.NBT.3 – Number & Operations in Base Ten

☐ How is four hundred ninety-two and fifty-six thousandths written as a numeral?

A   492.56

B   492.056

C   490.256

D   492.256

Common Core Standard 5.NBT.3 – Number & Operations in Base Ten

☐ Benjamin helped his grandmother move to a new house. He carried a box that weighed 9.7 pounds, another box that weighed 9.05 pounds, one that weighed 9.55 pounds, and the last one that weighed 9 pounds. How would you put the boxes in order from the lightest to the heaviest?

A   9 lbs, 9.7 lbs, 9.55 lbs, 9.05 lbs

B   9 lbs, 9.05 lbs, 9.55 lbs, 9.7 lbs

C   9.7 lbs, 9.55 lbs, 9.05 lbs, 9 lbs

D   9.7 lbs, 9.05 lbs, 9.55 lbs, 9 lbs

Common Core Standard 5.NBT.3 – Number & Operations in Base Ten

☐ How is six hundred thirty-nine and twenty thousandths written as a numeral?

A   639.20

B   639.200

C   639.020

D   639.920

Common Core Standard 5.NBT.3 – Number & Operations in Base Ten

☐ The circus sold 56.82 pounds of popcorn at the Orlando performance. When they went to Miami, they sold 55.99 pounds. In New York they sold 55.83 pounds, and 56.3 pounds in Philadelphia. How would you put the amounts of popcorn sold in order from the greatest to the least?

A   56.82 lbs, 55.83 lbs, 55.9 lbs, 56.3 lbs

B   56.82 lbs, 56.3 lbs, 55.99lbs, 55.83 lbs

C   55.83 lbs, 56.82 lbs, 56.3 lbs, 55.9 lbs

D   56.82 lbs, 56.3 lbs, 55.9 lbs, 55.83 lbs

Common Core Standard 5.NBT.3 – Number & Operations in Base Ten

☐ Jalen had two basketballs. One weighed 6.09 lbs, and the other one weighed 6.90 lbs. Which answer best describes the comparison of the his basketballs?

A   6.09 > 6.90

B   6.09 = 6.90

C   6.90 > 6.09

D   6.90 < 6.09

Common Core Standard 5.NBT.3 – Number & Operations in Base Ten

☐ How is two hundred seventy-six and thirty-eight thousandths written as a numeral?

A   276.038

B   276.638

C   276.083

D   276.38

Common Core Standard 5.NBT.3 – Number & Operations in Base Ten

☐ Some fifth grade students wanted to measure and compare their heights. Laura measures 58.75 inches, Stephen 58.9 inches, Gary 58.03 inches, and Maria's height is 58.1 inches. How should these heights be listed in order from the least to the greatest?

A   58.9 in, 58.75 in, 58.1 in, 58.03 in

B   58.9 in, 58.1 in, 58.75 in, 58.03 in

C   58.1 in, 58.9 in, 58.03 in, 58.75 in

D   58.03 in, 58.1 in, 58.75 in, 58.9 in

Common Core Standard 5.NBT.3 – Number & Operations in Base Ten

☐ Stan Musial's batting averages are listed below. Using his averages, which of the following statements is true?

A   Stan Musial's best year was 1950.

B   His average in 1950 was better than his 1943 average.

C   His lowest average was in 1948.

D   His average in 1948 was the best of these 4 averages.

Year	Average
1943	0.367
1946	0.365
1948	0.376
1950	0.346

Common Core Standard 5.NBT.3 – Number & Operations in Base Ten

☐ Andrew Chan participated in a sprint competition. He finished in fifty-four and forty-seven hundredths seconds. How did the scorekeeper write Andrew's time?

A   54 sec

B   45 sec

C   54.47 sec

D   47.54 sec

Name _____

Common Core Standard 5.NBT.3 – Number & Operations in Base Ten

☐ Babe Ruth's batting average was 0.315 in 1922 and 0.301 in 1933. Which of the following statements is true?

A   0.301 > 0.315

B   0.301 < 0.315

C   0.315 = 0.301

D   0.315 < 0.301

Common Core Standard 5.NBT.3 – Number & Operations in Base Ten

☐ Ethan's dog had 4 puppies last month. The puppies now weigh 2.8 kilograms, 3.3 kilograms, 2.09 kilograms, and 2.65 kilograms. What are the puppies' weights in order from the heaviest to the lightest?

A   2.8 kg, 3.3 kg, 2.09 kg, 2.65 kg

B   2.8 kg, 2.09 kg, 2.65 kg, 3.3 kg

C   2.09 kg, 2.65 kg, 2.8 kg, 3.3 kg

D   3.3 kg, 2.8 kg, 2.65 kg, 2.09 kg

Common Core Standard 5.NBT.3 – Number & Operations in Base Ten

☐ Mariah's class played a math game today. The students had to choose the correct sign to place between the two numbers Mr. Escobar wrote on the overhead projector. If Mr. Escobar wrote 0.043 and 0.004, which of the following statements would be correct?

A   0.043 = 0.004

B   0.043 < 0.004

C   0.004 < 0.043

D   0.004 > 0.043

Common Core Standard 5.NBT.4 – Number & Operations in Base Ten

☐ Carly's mother drives 37 miles back and forth to work every day. Which is the best estimate of how many miles she will have driven over a period of 6 days, if you round to the nearest hundreds place? Be sure to show your work.

A   300 mi

B   400 mi

C   200 mi

D   150 mi

Common Core Standard 5.NBT.4 – Number & Operations in Base Ten

☐ Brady and his father built a flower bed for his mother. They used timbers that measured 21.5 meters, 6.7 meters, 10.35 meters, and 9 meters in length. What is the length of all 4 timbers, if you round to the nearest tenths place? Be sure to show your work.

A   47.6 m

B   47 m

C   48 m

D   49 m

Common Core Standard 5.NBT.4 – Number & Operations in Base Ten

☐ Fernando is saving the money he earns when he rakes leaves for his neighbors. He charges an average of $14.75 for each lawn. If you round to the nearest tens place, how much money will Fernando have saved if he rakes 7 lawns? Be sure to show your work.

A $100

B $110

C $120

D $90

Common Core Standard 5.NBT.4 – Number & Operations in Base Ten

☐ Carmen checked a book out from the library that has 485 pages. After two days she had read 172 pages. How many pages does she has left to read if you round to the nearest tens place? Be sure to show your work.

A   290

B   300

C   310

D   320

Common Core Standard 5.NBT.4 – Number & Operations in Base Ten

☐ Marty bought items for her birthday party yesterday. She paid $3.57 for a package of candy, $7.20 for a box of cookies, and $5.59 for the party favors. How much did Marty spend before taxes if you round to the nearest tenths place? Be sure to show your work.

A $16.30

B $16.4

C $17

D $15

Common Core Standard 5.NBT.4 – Number & Operations in Base Ten

☐ Beverly measured each of her pet rabbits. The first one measured 12.234 cm, the second one measured 11.345 cm, and the third one measured 9.345 cm. How much did her rabbits measure in total if you round to the nearest hundredths place? Be sure to show your work.

A   32.93

B   33.00

C   32.90

D   32.92

Common Core Standard 5.NBT.4 – Number & Operations in Base Ten

☐ Mitchell bought a new science fiction DVD for $13.75. His father asked him to buy a package of blank DVDs so they could download some of their favorite movies. The package of blank DVD's costs $18.99. Rounding to the nearest tenths' place, how much was the total amount Mitchell spent on the DVDs? Be sure to show your work.

A $32.75

B $32.70

C $33.00

D $32.00

Common Core Standard 5.NBT.4 – Number & Operations in Base Ten

☐ Desiree collected postcards from cities in California. She has 775 in her collection. Round to the nearest ones place to find out how many postcards she would put in each box, if she puts the postcards in 4 boxes equally. Be sure to show your work.

A   193

B   195

C   194

D   193.8

Common Core Standard 5.NBT.4 – Number & Operations in Base Ten

☐ Trent's mother bought 4 shirts with a college football team logo on each. She paid $27.45, including tax, for each shirt. Round to the nearest hundreds' place to find out how much Trent's mother spent for the 4 shirts. Be sure to show your work.

A $109.9

B $110

C $108

D $100

Common Core Standard 5.NBT.4 – Number & Operations in Base Ten

☐ A bus makes 3 stops on its city route before it returns to the station. The first stop is 5.9953 kilometers from the station. The next stop is 0.9242 kilometers from the first stop and 3.4873 kilometers from the last stop. Round to the nearest thousandths' place to find out how far the bus traveled in total before it returned to the station. Be sure to show your work.

A   11 km

B   10.406 km

C   10.407 km

D   10.41 km

Common Core Standard 5.NBT.4 – Number & Operations in Base Ten

☐ Daniel and his friends have formed a band. They charge an average of $58.74 for each gig (performance by a band). Round to the nearest tenths' place to find out how much money they will earn if they schedule 3 gigs. Be sure to show your work.

A $176.20

B $177.00

C $176.000

D $180.00

Common Core Standard 5.NBT.4 – Number & Operations in Base Ten

☐ The zoo did a study on endangered animals. They studied a total of 393 elephants and 648 Bengal tigers. Rounding to the nearest tens place, find out how many more tigers than elephants were studied by the zoo. Be sure to show your work.

A   1000

B   250

C   300

D   260

Name _____

Common Core Standard 5.NBT.4 – Number & Operations in Base Ten

☐ Sara measured the distance from her house to several of her friends' houses. The distances were 11.448 miles to Carla's house, 6.679 miles to Meredith's house, 15.846 miles to Daphne's house, and 7 miles to Anita's house. Round to the nearest tenths' place to find the total distance to all of Sara's 4 friends' houses. Be sure to show your work.

A   41 mi

B   40.98 mi

C   40.97 mi

D   40.9 mi

Common Core Standard 5.NBT.4 – Number & Operations in Base Ten

☐ Mr. Franco spent $639.15 for a lawnmower and some gardening equipment at Elliot Hardware. Mr. Sanchez spent $866.94 for the same lawnmower and gardening equipment at Talley Hardware. Rounding to the nearest tenths' place, approximately how much money could Mr. Sanchez have saved if he had shopped at Elliot Hardware? Be sure to show your work.

A   More than $1500

B   Between $100 and $200

C   Between $200 and $300

D   Less than $100

Common Core Standard 5.NBT.4 – Number & Operations in Base Ten

☐ Alexander is keeping a record of the money he has spent on his pet dogs. Last month he spent $9.99 for a cage. This month he bought food that cost $5.89, and a book about raising dogs that cost $4.25. Rounding to the nearest tenths' place, how much money did Alexander spend in total? Be sure to show your work.

A $20

B $20.10

C $21.00

D $20.20

Name _____

Common Core Standard 5.NBT.4 – Number & Operations in Base Ten

☐ **Mr. Torres ordered 4 baskets of grapefruit. Each basket weighed 48.1578 pounds. Rounding to the nearest thousandths' place, how many pounds of grapefruit did Mr. Torres buy? Be sure to show your work.**

A   192.64 lbs.

B   192.60 lbs.

C   192.63 lbs.

D   192.631 lbs.

Common Core Standard 5.NBT.4 – Number & Operations in Base Ten

☐ **Troy mailed 3 packages from the post office for his mother. One package weighed 4.9348 pounds. The largest package weighed 6.5487 pounds, and the smallest package weighed 0.6159 pounds. Rounding to the nearest hundredths' place, how much was the total weight of the 3 packages? Be sure to show your work.**

A   12.01 lbs.

B   12.091 lbs.

C   12.10 lbs.

D   12.099 lbs.

Common Core Standard 5.NBT.4 – Number & Operations in Base Ten

☐ **Some of the students at Meeks Elementary are building cars for a competition at school. Jamal's car weighs 16.354 ounces. Felix built a car that weighs 12.629 ounces. Tony will enter the race with a car that weighs 14.082 ounces. The smallest car belongs to Max and weighs 9 ounces. Rounding to the nearest tenths' place, what is the total weight of all 4 cars? Be sure to show your work.**

A   52 oz.

B   52.07 oz.

C   52.1 oz.

D   52.06 oz.

Common Core Standard 5.NBT.4 – Number & Operations in Base Ten

☐ Baxter's Hamburger Shop ordered 77.258 pounds of meat for hamburgers last week. If they ordered the same amount for 52 weeks, which is the best estimate of the total amount of meat the hamburger shop ordered in one year? Round to the nearest ones' place to find the correct answer. Be sure to show your work.

A   4017 lbs.

B   4017.42 lbs.

C   4017.41 lbs.

D   4018 lbs.

Common Core Standard 5.NBT.4 – Number & Operations in Base Ten

☐ Baker Intermediate wants to buy new gym equipment. They had a bake sale that collected $285.18 in one weekend. The equipment will cost $920.94 if they buy everything they need. Rounding to the nearest hundredths' place, how much money do they still need to raise in order to to buy the gym equipment? Be sure to show your work.

A   Less than $200

B   Between $200 and $300

C   Between $300 and $400

D   More than $500

Common Core Standard 5.NBT.4 – Number & Operations in Base Ten

☐ Sydney takes piano lessons from Ms. Price. Ms. Price asked her to purchase 3 different pieces of sheet music for the recital. The sheet music costs $3.59, $2.99, and $5.05 each. Rounding to the nearest tenths' place, what is the cost for the sheet music before tax? Be sure to show your work.

A $ 12.00

B $ 11.00

C $ 11.6

D $ 11.70

Common Core Standard 5.NBT.4 – Number & Operations in Base Ten

☐ The service station earned $572.70 for changing oil in cars. If they changed oil in 29 cars, round to the nearest tenths' place to find the average cost for each oil change. Be sure to show your work.

A $19.00

B $20.00

C $19.7

D $19.01

Common Core Standard 5.NBT.4 – Number & Operations in Base Ten

☐ Dinner at the Cafe de Jon costs $27.59 for one person. Sam's Steakhouse charges $19.30 for dinner. If a person eats at both restaurants during one week, how much is the total amount? Round to the nearest ones place to find the correct answer. Be sure to show your work.

A $46.00

B $46.80

C $46.90

D $47.00

Common Core Standard 5.NBT.4 – Number & Operations in Base Ten

☐ The Christmas Tree store has a total of 48 Christmas trees. If each tree weighs 56.9098 pounds. How many pounds of Christmas trees do they have in total? Round to the nearest thousandths' place to find the correct answer. Be sure to show your work.

A   2731.671 lbs.

B   2731.67 lbs.

C   3000 lbs.

D   2731.68 lbs.

Common Core Standard 5.NBT.5 – Number & Operations in Base Ten

☐   **Solve the multiplication problem below. Be sure to show your work.**

5269
x 3254

Common Core Standard 5.NBT.5 – Number & Operations in Base Ten

☐   **Solve the multiplication problem below. Be sure to show your work.**

8457
x 128

Common Core Standard 5.NBT.5 – Number & Operations in Base Ten

☐   **Solve the multiplication problem below. Be sure to show your work.**

7239
x 6248

Common Core Standard 5.NBT.5 – Number & Operations in Base Ten

☐ **Solve the multiplication problem below. Be sure to show your work.**

$$4481$$
$$\underline{\times\ 552}$$

Common Core Standard 5.NBT.5 – Number & Operations in Base Ten

☐ **Solve the multiplication problem below. Be sure to show your work.**

$$2879$$
$$\underline{\times\ 2259}$$

Common Core Standard 5.NBT.5 – Number & Operations in Base Ten

☐ **Solve the multiplication problem below. Be sure to show your work.**

$$3222$$
$$\underline{\times\ 759}$$

Common Core Standard 5.NBT.5 – Number & Operations in Base Ten

☐ **Solve the multiplication problem below. Be sure to show your work.**

4385
x 2855

Common Core Standard 5.NBT.5 – Number & Operations in Base Ten

☐ **Solve the multiplication problem below. Be sure to show your work.**

7693
x 687

Common Core Standard 5.NBT.5 – Number & Operations in Base Ten

☐ **Solve the multiplication problem below. Be sure to show your work.**

5380
x 4384

Common Core Standard 5.NBT.5 – Number & Operations in Base Ten

☐ **Solve the multiplication problem below. Be sure to show your work.**

7703
x 495

Common Core Standard 5.NBT.5 – Number & Operations in Base Ten

☐ **Solve the multiplication problem below. Be sure to show your work.**

8971
x 7779

Common Core Standard 5.NBT.5 – Number & Operations in Base Ten

☐ **Solve the multiplication problem below. Be sure to show your work.**

5823
x 992

Common Core Standard 5.NBT.5 – Number & Operations in Base Ten

☐   **Solve the multiplication problem below. Be sure to show your work.**

8897
x 320

Common Core Standard 5.NBT.5 – Number & Operations in Base Ten

☐   **Solve the multiplication problem below. Be sure to show your work.**

2301
x 7736

Common Core Standard 5.NBT.5 – Number & Operations in Base Ten

☐   **Solve the multiplication problem below. Be sure to show your work.**

1483
x 888

Common Core Standard 5.NBT.5 – Number & Operations in Base Ten

☐   **Solve the multiplication problem below. Be sure to show your work.**

7541
x 8631

Common Core Standard 5.NBT.5 – Number & Operations in Base Ten

☐   **Solve the multiplication problem below. Be sure to show your work.**

5594
x 347

Common Core Standard 5.NBT.5 – Number & Operations in Base Ten

☐   **Solve the multiplication problem below. Be sure to show your work.**

3971
x 9327

Common Core Standard 5.NBT.5 – Number & Operations in Base Ten

☐ **Solve the multiplication problem below. Be sure to show your work.**

7944
x 299

Common Core Standard 5.NBT.5 – Number & Operations in Base Ten

☐ **Solve the multiplication problem below. Be sure to show your work.**

4936
x 8947

Common Core Standard 5.NBT.5 – Number & Operations in Base Ten

☐ **Solve the multiplication problem below. Be sure to show your work.**

3339
x 241

Common Core Standard 5.NBT.5 – Number & Operations in Base Ten

☐ **Solve the multiplication problem below. Be sure to show your work.**

6122
x 7074

Common Core Standard 5.NBT.5 – Number & Operations in Base Ten

☐ **Solve the multiplication problem below. Be sure to show your work.**

3416
x 883

Common Core Standard 5.NBT.5 – Number & Operations in Base Ten

☐ **Solve the multiplication problem below. Be sure to show your work.**

9693
x 9999

Common Core Standard 5.NBT.6 – Number & Operations in Base Ten

☐   **Solve the division problem below. Be sure to show your work.**

$$1{,}302 \div 21 = \boxed{}$$

Common Core Standard 5.NBT.6 – Number & Operations in Base Ten

☐   **Solve the division problem below. Be sure to show your work.**

$$96\overline{)7{,}104}$$

Common Core Standard 5.NBT.6 – Number & Operations in Base Ten

☐   **Solve the division problem below. Be sure to show your work.**

6,688 divided by 76 equals _____.

Common Core Standard 5.NBT.6 – Number & Operations in Base Ten

☐   **Marcos wants to find out his favorite baseball player's earned run average (ERA). To calculate ERA, you must divide total innings pitched by total earned runs. Marcos' favorite player pitched 1943 total innings and had 67 earned runs. What was his favorite player's ERA? Be sure to show your work.**

      A   34

      B   29

      C   26

      D   34

Common Core Standard 5.NBT.6 – Number & Operations in Base Ten

☐   **Solve the division problem below. Be sure to show your work.**

$$2,752 \div 32 = \boxed{}$$

Common Core Standard 5.NBT.6 – Number & Operations in Base Ten

☐   **Natasha's family flew around the country for a total of 2,890 miles. If it took her family 34 days to fly around the country, how many miles was each trip? Be sure to show your work.**

      A   65

      B   75

      C   85

      D   95

Common Core Standard 5.NBT.6 – Number & Operations in Base Ten

☐ Solve the division problem below. Be sure to show your work.

$$3{,}995 \div 85 = \boxed{}$$

Common Core Standard 5.NBT.6 – Number & Operations in Base Ten

☐ Solve the division problem below. Be sure to show your work.

$$1{,}216 / 64 = \boxed{}$$

Common Core Standard 5.NBT.6 – Number & Operations in Base Ten

☐ Ramen has collected 5,529 stamps. It took him 97 days to collect all the stamps. On average, how many stamps did he buy each day? Be sure to show your work.

A   56

B   59

C   58

D   57

Common Core Standard 5.NBT.6 – Number & Operations in Base Ten

☐ **Solve the division problem below. Be sure to show your work.**

$$6,935 \div 73 = \boxed{}$$

Common Core Standard 5.NBT.6 – Number & Operations in Base Ten

☐ **Solve the division problem below. Be sure to show your work.**

$$54\overline{)4,482}$$

Common Core Standard 5.NBT.6 – Number & Operations in Base Ten

☐ **Solve the division problem below. Be sure to show your work.**

$$3,410 / 55 = \boxed{}$$

Name _____

Common Core Standard 5.NBT.6 – Number & Operations in Base Ten

☐ **Katie volunteered at the local food bank to help sort food into boxes. There were 1,173 pieces of fruit that needed to be separated into 17 boxes. How many pieces of fruit were in each box equally? Be sure to show your work.**

> A   69
>
> B   70
>
> C   60
>
> D   67

Common Core Standard 5.NBT.6 – Number & Operations in Base Ten

☐ **Solve the division problem below. Be sure to show your work.**

$$2{,}808 \div 78 = \boxed{}$$

Common Core Standard 5.NBT.6 – Number & Operations in Base Ten

☐ **A florist needed to put 2,368 flowers into 74 vases. How many flowers were in each vase equally? Be sure to show your work.**

> A   40
>
> B   33
>
> C   32
>
> D   34

Common Core Standard 5.NBT.6 – Number & Operations in Base Ten

☐ **Solve the division problem below. Be sure to show your work.**

$$6,391 \div 83 = \boxed{}$$

Common Core Standard 5.NBT.6 – Number & Operations in Base Ten

☐ **Solve the division problem below. Be sure to show your work.**

$$37\overline{)2,294}$$

Common Core Standard 5.NBT.6 – Number & Operations in Base Ten

☐ **Solve the division problem below. Be sure to show your work.**

$$4,672 / 73 = \boxed{}$$

Common Core Standard 5.NBT.6 – Number & Operations in Base Ten

☐ Celina Public Library has 4,402 books that need to be sorted on each of the 62 shelves. How many books are on each shelf if they are sorted equally? Be sure to show your work.

A   72

B   69

C   70

D   71

Common Core Standard 5.NBT.6 – Number & Operations in Base Ten

☐ Solve the division problem below. Be sure to show your work.

$$6{,}786 \div 87 = \boxed{}$$

Common Core Standard 5.NBT.6 – Number & Operations in Base Ten

☐ Demetris scored 2,479 goals last season. If he played 67 games, what was the average number of goals he scored during each game? Be sure to show your work.

A   40 points per game

B   37 points per game

C   38 points per game

D   36 points per game

Common Core Standard 5.NBT.6 – Number & Operations in Base Ten

☐   **Solve the division problem below. Be sure to show your work.**

$$4,056 \div 78 = \boxed{}$$

Common Core Standard 5.NBT.6 – Number & Operations in Base Ten

☐   **Solve the division problem below. Be sure to show your work.**

$$2,125 \,/\, 85 = \boxed{}$$

Common Core Standard 5.NBT.6 – Number & Operations in Base Ten

☐   **Solve the division problem below. Be sure to show your work.**

1,156 divided by 34 equals _____.

Common Core Standard 5.NBT.7 – Number & Operations in Base Ten

☐ Mrs. Navarro bought her three children new shoes. Alejandro's shoes cost $45.99, Maria's tennis shoes cost $39.95, and Anita's shoes cost $57.25. What was the total amount Mrs. Navarro spent? Be sure to show your work.

A $243.19

B $143.19

C $121.09

D $133.19

Common Core Standard 5.NBT.7 – Number & Operations in Base Ten

☐ During a paper drive James collected 14.5 kilograms of newspapers each day. How many kilograms of newspapers did James collect in one week? Be sure to show your work.

E   72.5 kg

F   130.5 kg

G   101.5 kg

H   118.4 kg

Common Core Standard 5.NBT.7 – Number & Operations in Base Ten

☐ It snowed a total of 28.87 inches in two days. On Tuesday 12.15 inches of snow fell. How many inches of snow fell on Monday? Be sure to show your work.

I   15.87 in

J   16.71 in

K   17.72 in

L   16.72 in

Common Core Standard 5.NBT.7 – Number & Operations in Base Ten

☐ Jennifer bought a package of pencils at a discount store for $2.49. She then used a five dollar bill to pay for the pencils. How much money did Jennifer have left over? Be sure to show your work.

A $3.49

B $2.50

C $2.51

D $3.51

Common Core Standard 5.NBT.7 – Number & Operations in Base Ten

☐ Four fifth grade girl-classes competed in a sack race. The total time for all four fifth grade girl-classes was 80.8 seconds. The total time for the fifth grade boys was 74.8. What was the average time for each of the fifth grade girl-class? Be sure to show your work.

A   20.2 sec

B   18.7 sec

C   80.8 sec

D   74.8 sec

Common Core Standard 5.NBT.7 – Number & Operations in Base Ten

☐ Greg's team walked 5.3 miles at the walkathon. Brandy's team walked 4.75 miles, and Hector's team walked 6.84 miles. Robin's team walked only 2.7 miles because one of their members turned her ankle. How many miles in all did the 4 teams walk? Be sure to show your work.

A   19.49 miles

B   12.39 miles

C   19.59 miles

D   18.59 miles

Name _____

Common Core Standard 5.NBT.7 – Number & Operations in Base Ten

☐ Lauren bought some books at the book fair. She spent $5.72 for a book about dogs. She also spent $7.99 for a puzzle book, and $3.48 for a book of riddles. If she used a $20 bill to pay for all her books, how much money did she have left? Be sure to show your work.

A $17.19

B $2.81

C $3.81

D $17.09

Common Core Standard 5.NBT.7 – Number & Operations in Base Ten

☐ Brian's dog weighs 19.3 pounds. Felicia's cat weighs 4.8 pounds. How much more does Brian's dog weigh than Felicia's cat? Be sure to show your work.

A   24.1 lbs

B   92.64 lbs

C   14.5 lbs

D   14.19 lbs

Common Core Standard 5.NBT.7 – Number & Operations in Base Ten

☐ Mr. Franco purchased items for his camping trip. He bought 2 flashlights for $17.95 each, a first-aid kit for $3.59, and 2 cans of mosquito spray for $2.34 each, not including tax. How much did the items cost, not including tax? Be sure to show your work.

A $44.17

B $23.88

C $27.88

D $142.15

Common Core Standard 5.NBT.7 – Number & Operations in Base Ten

[ ]   Jeremy earned $30 for baby-sitting his little brother. He wants to buy a game that costs $5.75, a CD that costs $7.99, and a book that costs $3.87. All amounts included tax. How much money will Jeremy spend, if he buys all 3 items? Be sure to show your work.

A $47.61

B $17.61

C $18.61

D $17.51

Common Core Standard 5.NBT.7 – Number & Operations in Base Ten

[ ]   It takes Marcie 7.38 minutes to walk to school. Her friend Carlos rides his bike to school in 8 minutes. If Carlos rides his bike 5 times a week to and from school, how much time does he ride in total?   Be sure to show your work.

A   36.9 mins.

B   40 mins.

C   80 mins.

D   120 mins.

Common Core Standard 5.NBT.7 – Number & Operations in Base Ten

[ ]   Gabriel saved $9.73 from his allowance last month and $6.47 from his allowance this month to buy Christmas gifts. How much money has he saved? Be sure to show your work.

A $16.30

B $15.10

C $15.20

D $16.20

Common Core Standard 5.NBT.7 – Number & Operations in Base Ten

☐ DeSean rushed for 1548 yards as a running back for his football team. If he played 13 games, how many yards did he average per game? Round to the nearest hundredths' place to find the correct answer. Be sure to show your work.

A   119.08 yards

B   119.07 yards

C   119.1 yards

D   100 yards

Common Core Standard 5.NBT.7 – Number & Operations in Base Ten

☐ Benjamin took a twenty dollar bill to the store. He bought a shirt for $15.79. The sales tax was $1.28. How much change should he receive? Be sure to show your work.

A $13.03

B $2.93

C $2.03

D $4.21

Common Core Standard 5.NBT.7 – Number & Operations in Base Ten

☐ Maggie's dad built a new garden planter. The length of the planter is 109.275 feet, and the width is 89.578 feet. What is the difference between the length and the width of the garden planter? Be sure to show your work.

A   19.797 ft

B   19.697 ft

C   20.697 ft

D   20.707 ft

Common Core Standard 5.NBT.7 – Number & Operations in Base Ten

☐ Ally's father cut a piece of wire 13.95 feet long and another piece 15.39 feet long. The roll of wire contained 36.7 feet before her father cut the 2 pieces. How much wire is left on the roll? Be sure to show your work.

A   64 ft.

B   7.43 ft.

C   7.36 ft.

D   7.35 ft.

Common Core Standard 5.NBT.7 – Number & Operations in Base Ten

☐ Three boys sold tickets for a raffle. The table shows the number of tickets sold and amount of money earned. What was the total number of tickets sold by the boys? Be sure to show your work.

A $259.00

B   74

C   333

D $333.00

Name	Number of Tickets Sold	Amount Earned
Andrew	21	$73.50
Tomas	34	$119.00
Mack	19	$66.50

Common Core Standard 5.NBT.7 – Number & Operations in Base Ten

☐ Three stores had a sale on markers. Store A sold a box of markers for $2.37, Store B sold the same box of markers for $2.89, and Store C had the box of markers priced at $1.99. If Erin bought a box of markers from the store with the lowest price and paid for them with a $5 bill, how much change should she have received? Be sure to show your work.

A $2.25

B $2.63

C $3.01

D $4.99

Common Core Standard 5.NBT.7 – Number & Operations in Base Ten

☐ Kylie placed an order on the internet for some DVDs. She bought an action movie for $9.72, a cartoon DVD for $7.99, and a romance DVD for $6.25. What was the total amount she spent on the DVDs? Be sure to show your work.

A $22.96

B $23.96

C $22.86

D $23.86

Common Core Standard 5.NBT.7 – Number & Operations in Base Ten

☐ The first baby born in the new year weighed 2.7 kilograms. The next three babies weighed 3.9 kilograms, 3.5 kilograms, and 4.13 kilograms. How much did the 4 babies weigh all together? Be sure to show your work.

A   16.33 kg.

B   24.23 kg.

C   144 kg.

D   14.23 kg.

Common Core Standard 5.NBT.7 – Number & Operations in Base Ten

☐ Romero's father cut 4 pieces of wire for the fence he is building. He cut a piece 3.5 meters long, another piece 4.9 meters long, and two pieces that measured 7.3 meters each. What was the combined length of the 4 pieces of wire? Be sure to show your work.

A   23.9 meters

B   16 meters

C   23.4 meters

D   23 meters

Common Core Standard 5.NBT.7 – Number & Operations in Base Ten

☐ Edgar rode his bicycle 13.8 miles each day to school. If he rode his bike 17 times in the month of March, how many miles did he ride in March? Be sure to show your work.

A   325 miles

B   231.20 miles

C   220.80 miles

D   234.60 miles

Common Core Standard 5.NBT.7 – Number & Operations in Base Ten

☐ Brooks Grocery store has 125.98 kilograms of vegetables to sort through. If the store has 13 different kinds of vegetables, what is the weight of each type of vegetable in kilograms equally? Round to the nearest hundredths' place to find the correct answer. Be sure to show your work.

A   9.70 kg.

B   9.69 kg.

C   10 kg.

D   9.68 kg.

Common Core Standard 5.NBT.7 – Number & Operations in Base Ten

☐ Levi walked 4.53 miles on Monday and 3.99 miles on Tuesday. How much farther did he walk on Monday than on Tuesday? Be sure to show your work.

A   1.54 miles

B   0.54 miles

C   8.52 miles

D   1.64 miles

Common Core Standard 5.NF.1 – Number & Operations - Fractions

☐   **Solve the fraction below to find the correct answer. Be sure to show your work.**

$$2\frac{8}{7} + 3\frac{11}{21} =$$

Common Core Standard 5.NF.1 – Number & Operations – Fractions

☐   **Solve the fraction below to find the correct answer. Be sure to show your work.**

$$20\frac{1}{2} - 9\frac{3}{6} =$$

Common Core Standard 5.NF.1 – Number & Operations - Fractions

☐   **Solve the fraction below to find the correct answer. Be sure to show your work.**

$$12\frac{10}{12} + 9\frac{2}{7} =$$

Common Core Standard 5.NF.1 – Number & Operations - Fractions

☐ **Solve the fraction below to find the correct answer. Be sure to show your work.**

$$9\frac{8}{12} - 8\frac{1}{2} =$$

Common Core Standard 5.NF.1 – Number & Operations – Fractions

☐ **Solve the fraction below to find the correct answer. Be sure to show your work.**

$$13\frac{2}{5} + 6\frac{2}{11} =$$

Common Core Standard 5.NF.1 – Number & Operations – Fractions

☐ **Solve the fraction below to find the correct answer. Be sure to show your work.**

$$7\frac{1}{12} - 6\frac{1}{7} =$$

Name _____

Common Core Standard 5.NF.1 – Number & Operations - Fractions

☐ Solve the fraction below to find the correct answer. Be sure to show your work.

$$\frac{46}{27} - \frac{11}{9} =$$

Common Core Standard 5.NF.1 – Number & Operations – Fractions

☐ Solve the fraction below to find the correct answer. Be sure to show your work.

$$37\frac{47}{32} + 23\frac{6}{16} =$$

Common Core Standard 5.NF.1 – Number & Operations – Fractions

☐ Solve the fraction below to find the correct answer. Be sure to show your work.

$$14\frac{2}{9} - 3\frac{9}{10} =$$

Common Core Standard 5.NF.1 – Number & Operations - Fractions

☐ **Solve the fraction below to find the correct answer. Be sure to show your work.**

$$16\frac{4}{9} + 20\frac{2}{4} =$$

Common Core Standard 5.NF.1 – Number & Operations – Fractions

☐ **Solve the fraction below to find the correct answer. Be sure to show your work.**

$$19\frac{3}{9} - 4\frac{4}{8} =$$

Common Core Standard 5.NF.1 – Number & Operations - Fractions

☐ **Solve the fraction below to find the correct answer. Be sure to show your work.**

$$9\frac{1}{7} + 18\frac{2}{10} =$$

Common Core Standard 5.NF.1 – Number & Operations - Fractions

☐ **Solve the fraction below to find the correct answer. Be sure to show your work.**

$$3\frac{4}{6} + 12\frac{1}{3} =$$

Common Core Standard 5.NF.1 – Number & Operations – Fractions

☐ **Solve the fraction below to find the correct answer. Be sure to show your work.**

$$18\frac{4}{9} - 15\frac{3}{7} =$$

Common Core Standard 5.NF.1 – Number & Operations – Fractions

☐ **Solve the fraction below to find the correct answer. Be sure to show your work.**

$$6\frac{4}{8} + 9\frac{1}{9} =$$

Common Core Standard 5.NF.1 – Number & Operations - Fractions

☐ **Solve the fraction below to find the correct answer. Be sure to show your work.**

$$10\frac{2}{7} - 8\frac{1}{11} =$$

Common Core Standard 5.NF.1 – Number & Operations – Fractions

☐ **Solve the fraction below to find the correct answer. Be sure to show your work.**

$$9\frac{1}{6} + 5\frac{4}{8} =$$

Common Core Standard 5.NF.1 – Number & Operations – Fractions

☐ **Solve the fraction below to find the correct answer. Be sure to show your work.**

$$6\frac{3}{5} - 3\frac{1}{10} =$$

Common Core Standard 5.NF.1 – Number & Operations - Fractions

☐   Solve the fraction below to find the correct answer. Be sure to show your work.

$$2\frac{31}{21} + 3\frac{21}{42} =$$

Common Core Standard 5.NF.1 – Number & Operations – Fractions

☐   Solve the fraction below to find the correct answer. Be sure to show your work.

$$18\frac{4}{10} - 14\frac{11}{12} =$$

Common Core Standard 5.NF.1 – Number & Operations – Fractions

☐   Solve the fraction below to find the correct answer. Be sure to show your work.

$$2\frac{2}{12} + 9\frac{3}{8} =$$

Common Core Standard 5.NF.1 – Number & Operations - Fractions

☐ **Solve the fraction below to find the correct answer. Be sure to show your work.**

$$\frac{8}{15} - \frac{5}{30} =$$

Common Core Standard 5.NF.1 – Number & Operations – Fractions

☐ **Solve the fraction below to find the correct answer. Be sure to show your work.**

$$9\frac{9}{11} + 3\frac{1}{4} =$$

Common Core Standard 5.NF.1 – Number & Operations – Fractions

☐ **Solve the fraction below to find the correct answer. Be sure to show your work.**

$$14\frac{4}{11} - 4\frac{9}{33} =$$

Common Core Standard 5.NF.2 – Number & Operations – Fractions

☐ Griffin helped the school librarian for two weeks. The first week he worked $6\frac{1}{2}$ hours, and $3\frac{1}{4}$ hours the next week. Which of the number sentences can be used to find how much longer he worked the first week compared to the second week?

A $\quad 6\frac{1}{2} - 3\frac{1}{4} = 3\frac{1}{6}$

C $\quad 6\frac{2}{4} - 3\frac{1}{4} = 3\frac{1}{4}$

B $\quad 6\frac{2}{4} + 3\frac{1}{4} = 3\frac{3}{4}$

D $\quad 6\frac{1}{2} + 3\frac{1}{4} = 9$

Common Core Standard 5.NF.2 – Number & Operations – Fractions

☐ Mack read $2\frac{3}{4}$ chapters of a book he bought yesterday. If he read $1\frac{2}{4}$ chapters today, how many chapters has he read in 2 days? Be sure to show your work.

A $\quad 1\frac{1}{4}$

B $\quad 2\frac{1}{4}$

C $\quad 3\frac{1}{4}$

D $\quad 4\frac{1}{4}$

Common Core Standard 5.NF.2 – Number & Operations – Fraction

☐ Maria ate $\frac{5}{9}$ of a pizza and her brother ate $\frac{2}{9}$ of the same pizza. What fraction of the entire pizza did they eat together?

A $\quad \frac{2}{9}$

B $\quad \frac{7}{9}$

C $\quad \frac{3}{9}$

D $\quad \frac{7}{18}$

Common Core Standard 5.NF.2 – Number & Operations – Fractions

☐ Wendy bought a box of candy for her mother. If her mother has eaten $\frac{5}{8}$ of the candy, what fraction of candy is left? Be sure to show your work.

A $\frac{3}{8}$ C $\frac{2}{8}$

B $\frac{9}{8}$ D $\frac{4}{8}$

Common Core Standard 5.NF.2 – Number & Operations – Fractions

☐ Wyatt's grandfather bought 10 sacks of grass seed to put on his lawn. He spread $\frac{3}{10}$ of the sacks on Friday and $\frac{4}{10}$ of the sacks of grass seed on Saturday. If he spreads the remaining sacks next week, what fraction represents the remaining sacks? Be sure to show your work.

A $\frac{7}{10}$ C $\frac{3}{10}$

B $\frac{6}{10}$ D $\frac{7}{10}$

Common Core Standard 5.NF.2 – Number & Operations – Fractions

☐ William has completed $\frac{3}{8}$ of his homework, and Brent has completed $\frac{7}{8}$ of his homework. What fraction of his homework does Brent still need to complete? Be sure to show your work.

A $\frac{5}{8}$ C $\frac{10}{16}$

B $\frac{10}{8}$ D $\frac{1}{8}$

Common Core Standard 5.NF.2 – Number & Operations – Fractions

[ ] Jason saved his allowance to buy a video game. When he priced the game, it cost $15. He has only saved $\frac{3}{5}$ of the cost of the game. What fraction below represents the amount he needs to save to buy the video game? Be sure to show your work.

A $\frac{3}{5}$ C $\frac{5}{3}$

B $\frac{45}{75}$ D $\frac{2}{5}$

Common Core Standard 5.NF.2 – Number & Operations – Fractions

[ ] At the Halloween Bazaar, $\frac{6}{9}$ of the students participated in the Halloween Dance and $\frac{2}{9}$ of the students participated in Costume Contest. How many more students participated in the Halloween Dance than the Costume Contest? Be sure to show your work.

A $\frac{4}{9}$ C $\frac{8}{9}$

B $\frac{8}{18}$ D $\frac{1}{9}$

Common Core Standard 5.NF.2 – Number & Operations – Fractions

[ ] Michael drank $\frac{2}{6}$ of chocolate milk in the morning and $\frac{3}{6}$ of chocolate milk in the evening. How much chocolate milk did Michael drink in all? Be sure to show your work.

A $\frac{1}{6}$ C $\frac{5}{6}$

B $\frac{5}{12}$ D 1

Common Core Standard 5.NF.2 – Number & Operations – Fractions

☐ Kimberly made a cake for her mother's birthday. She used $\frac{4}{12}$ of a cup of sugar, $\frac{1}{12}$ of a cup of baking powder, $\frac{3}{12}$ of a cup of milk, and $\frac{2}{12}$ of a cup of chocolate. How many cups of ingredients did she use for the cake? Be sure to show your work.

A $\frac{24}{12}$ C $\frac{9}{12}$

B $\frac{11}{12}$ D $\frac{10}{12}$

Common Core Standard 5.NF.2 – Number & Operations – Fractions

☐ Ismael bought $\frac{2}{7}$ bag of oranges and $\frac{5}{7}$ bag of apples. How many more bags of apples than oranges did Ismael buy? Be sure to show your work.

A   1   C $\frac{10}{49}$

B $\frac{3}{7}$ D $\frac{2}{7}$

Common Core Standard 5.NF.2 – Number & Operations – Fractions

☐ The school bus drove $\frac{2}{3}$ of a kilometer from school to Shelby's house. It then drove $\frac{4}{15}$ of a kilometer from Shelby's house to Gareth's house. How many kilometers did the school bus drive in total? Be sure to show your work.

A $\frac{14}{15}$ C $\frac{6}{18}$

B $\frac{2}{12}$ D $\frac{12}{15}$

Common Core Standard 5.NF.2 – Number & Operations – Fractions

☐ Andy's mother made some coffee in the morning. She used $\frac{1}{7}$ of a spoon of coffee and $\frac{2}{7}$ of a spoon of sugar. How many spoons of ingredients did Andy's mother use for the coffee? Be sure to show your work.

A $\frac{2}{49}$ C $\frac{1}{7}$

B $\frac{3}{14}$ D $\frac{3}{7}$

Common Core Standard 5.NF.2 – Number & Operations – Fractions

☐ Jeffry painted a picture for his art project. To paint his picture, he used $\frac{1}{10}$ of a red color, $\frac{3}{10}$ of a yellow color, and $\frac{2}{10}$ of a green color. How much paint did Jeffry use in all to finish his picture? Be sure to show your work.

A $\frac{6}{30}$ C $\frac{7}{10}$

B $\frac{6}{10}$ D $\frac{1}{2}$

Common Core Standard 5.NF.2 – Number & Operations - Fractions

☐ Jamarcus finished his ice cream in $\frac{3}{6}$ of an hour, and his brother Jamal finished his ice cream in $\frac{1}{6}$ of an hour. Who finished their ice cream first?

A   Jamal   C   They both tied

B   Jamarcus   D   Neither

Common Core Standard 5.NF.2 – Number & Operations – Fractions

☐ Cherie made cupcakes for her class. She used $\frac{4}{12}$ of a cup milk, $\frac{2}{12}$ of a cup of sugar, and $\frac{1}{12}$ of a cup of baking powder. How many cups of ingredients did she use to make the cupcakes? Be sure to show your work.

A $\quad \frac{7}{12}$

C $\quad \frac{8}{12}$

B $\quad \frac{1}{2}$

D $\quad \frac{2}{3}$

Common Core Standard 5.NF.2 – Number & Operations – Fractions

☐ Sherrill went to the sports store and bought $\frac{3}{8}$ box of baseballs and $\frac{1}{8}$ box of tennis balls. How many more baseballs did Sherrill buy than tennis balls? Be sure to show your work.

A $\quad \frac{4}{16}$

C $\quad \frac{1}{2}$

B $\quad \frac{3}{8}$

D $\quad \frac{1}{4}$

Common Core Standard 5.NF.2 – Number & Operations – Fractions

☐ Sophie wants to make a cake for her grandmother. She put $\frac{3}{7}$ of red icing and $\frac{1}{7}$ white icing on the cake. How many red and white icing did she put on the cake? Be sure to show your work.

A $\quad \frac{4}{14}$

C $\quad \frac{4}{7}$

B $\quad \frac{3}{7}$

D $\quad \frac{3}{49}$

Common Core Standard 5.NF.2 – Number & Operations – Fractions

☐ Remi grew $\frac{4}{6}$ of an inch during one month, and his friend Gustav grew $\frac{1}{2}$ of an inch. How much more did Remi grow than Gustav? Be sure to show your work.

A $\frac{1}{2}$ C $\frac{1}{3}$

B $\frac{1}{6}$ D $\frac{7}{6}$

Common Core Standard 5.NF 2 – Number & Operations – Fractions

☐ At a pet store, $\frac{7}{10}$ of the puppies are black and $\frac{3}{10}$ of the puppies are white. If you have 10 puppies in total, how many more black puppies than white puppies are there? Be sure to show your work.

A   4   C $\frac{21}{10}$

B   1   D $\frac{2}{5}$

Common Core Standard 5.NF.2 – Number & Operations – Fractions

☐ Marco's Pizzeria uses $\frac{3}{8}$ of a cup of cheese, $\frac{1}{8}$ of a cup of butter, and $\frac{5}{8}$ of its secret sauce to make a cheese pizza. How many cups of ingredients do they use for the cheese pizza? Be sure to show your work.

A $\frac{15}{8}$ C $\frac{9}{8}$

B $\frac{10}{8}$ D $\frac{1}{8}$

Common Core Standard 5.NF.2 – Number & Operations – Fractions

☐ In Julio's class, $\frac{3}{5}$ of all students have a brother, and $\frac{1}{5}$ have a sister. How many more students in Julio's class have only a brother? Be sure to show your work.

A $\frac{4}{5}$ C $\frac{4}{10}$

B $\frac{3}{25}$ D $\frac{2}{5}$

Common Core Standard 5.NF.2 – Number & Operations – Fractions

☐ June received some candies. $\frac{2}{15}$ of them are green, $\frac{6}{15}$ of them are yellow, $\frac{3}{15}$ of them are red, and the rest are blue. How many candies are blue? Be sure to show your work.

A $\frac{4}{15}$ C $\frac{11}{15}$

B $\frac{1}{5}$ D $\frac{6}{15}$

Common Core Standard 5.NF.2 – Number & Operations – Fractions

☐ Heindrick has $\frac{5}{9}$ football cards and $\frac{1}{3}$ baseballs cards. How many more football cards than baseball cards does Heindrick have? Be sure to show your work.

A $\frac{2}{3}$ C $\frac{2}{9}$

B $\frac{1}{2}$ D $\frac{5}{81}$

Common Core Standard 5.NF.3 – Number & Operations – Fractions

☐ **What fraction best describes the shaded model below?**

A $\dfrac{2}{7}$ C $\dfrac{3}{8}$

B $\dfrac{3}{7}$ D $\dfrac{4}{7}$

Common Core Standard 5.NF.3 – Number & Operations – Fractions

☐ **If 3 students want to divide 41 coloring paper sheets equally, how many coloring paper sheets will each student receive? What two whole numbers would the correct answer lie between? Be sure to show your work.**

A   38; 37 and 39   C $13\dfrac{2}{3}$; 13 and 14

B $10\dfrac{1}{4}$; 10 and 11   D $20\dfrac{1}{2}$; 20 and 21

Common Core Standard 5.NF.3 – Number & Operations – Fractions

☐ **What fraction best describes the shaded model below?**

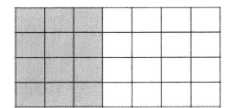

A $\dfrac{6}{7}$ C $\dfrac{3}{7}$

B $\dfrac{13}{28}$ D $\dfrac{15}{28}$

Name _____

DIAGNOSTIC

Common Core Standard 5.NF.3 – Number & Operations – Fractions

☐   **If Mikaila and Arin want to divide 17 cupcakes equally, how many cupcakes will each girl receive? What two whole numbers would the correct answer lie between? Be sure to show your work.**

A $8\frac{1}{2}$; 8 and 9   C $5\frac{7}{10}$; 5 and 6

B   17; 16 and 18   D $9\frac{1}{2}$; 9 and 10

Common Core Standard 5.NF.3 – Number & Operations – Fractions

☐   **What fraction best describes the shaded hearts below?**

A $\frac{3}{4}$ C $\frac{5}{8}$

B $\frac{3}{8}$ D $\frac{1}{2}$

Common Core Standard 5.NF.3 – Number & Operations – Fractions

☐   **If 5 persons want to divide 23 lb of sugar equally, how many lbs of sugar will each person receive? What two whole numbers would the correct answer lie between? Be sure to show your work.**

A   23; 22 and 24   C $5\frac{2}{5}$; 5 and 6

B $4\frac{3}{5}$; 4 and 5   D $18\frac{1}{2}$; 18 and 19

©Teachers' Treasures Publishing

Page 98

Name _____

Common Core Standard 5.NF.3 – Number & Operations – Fractions

☐ Shane, Greg, Herb, and John want to divide 26 baseballs equally. How many baseballs will each boy receive? What two whole numbers would the correct answer lie between? Be sure to show your work.

A $8\frac{3}{5}$; 8 and 9   C $6\frac{1}{2}$; 7 and 8

B $5\frac{3}{5}$; 5 and 6   D $6\frac{1}{2}$; 6 and 7

Common Core Standard 5.NF.3 – Number & Operations – Fractions

☐ What fraction best describes the shaded model below?

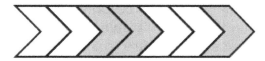

A $\frac{1}{2}$ C $\frac{4}{7}$

B $\frac{3}{7}$ D $\frac{5}{7}$

Common Core Standard 5.NF.3 – Number & Operations – Fractions

☐ If 4 friends want to divide 38 liters of water equally, how many liters of water will each friend receive? What two whole numbers would the correct answer lie between? Be sure to show your work.

A   19; 18 and 20   C $9\frac{1}{2}$; 9 and 10

B $4\frac{1}{4}$; 4 and 5   D $19\frac{1}{2}$; 19 and 20

Name _____

Common Core Standard 5.NF.3 – Number & Operations – Fractions

☐ **What fraction best describes the shaded model below?**

A $\frac{5}{9}$ C $\frac{4}{7}$

B $\frac{1}{2}$ D $\frac{4}{9}$

Common Core Standard 5.NF.3 – Number & Operations – Fractions

☐ **If 7 teams were to divide 66 players equally between teams, how many players will be on each team? What two whole numbers would the correct answer lie between? Be sure to show your work.**

A $7\frac{1}{3}$; 7 and 8   C $8\frac{1}{4}$; 8 and 9

B $9\frac{3}{7}$; 9 and 10   D   11; 10 and 12

Common Core Standard 5.NF.3 – Number & Operations – Fractions

☐ **If 6 workers want to divide $62 equally, how many dollars will each worker receive? What two whole numbers would the correct answer lie between? Be sure to show your work.**

A   62; 61 and 63   C $6\frac{2}{3}$; 5 and 7

B $10\frac{1}{3}$; 10 and 11   D $9\frac{3}{4}$; 9 and 10

Name _____

Common Core Standard 5.NF.3 – Number & Operations – Fractions

☐ Jules prepared punch juice for her father's birthday party. She used 10 kg of pineapple juice and 20 kg of apple juice. She has a measuring cup marked in units of a cup. How many times should she fill the measuring cup with pineapple juice using the rule 1 kg = 10 cups? Be sure to show your work.

A   100   C   110

B   120   D   90

Common Core Standard 5.NF.3 – Number & Operations – Fractions

☐ What fraction best describes the shaded model below?

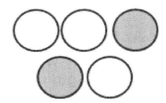

A $\frac{4}{5}$ C $\frac{3}{5}$

B $\frac{2}{5}$ D $\frac{1}{5}$

Common Core Standard 5.NF.3 – Number & Operations – Fractions

☐ What fraction best describes the shaded model below?

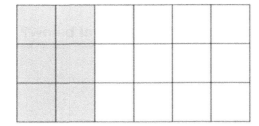

A $\frac{1}{3}$ C $\frac{1}{2}$

B $\frac{2}{3}$ D $\frac{3}{4}$

Common Core Standard 5.NF.3 – Number & Operations – Fractions

☐ **What fraction best describes the shaded model below?**

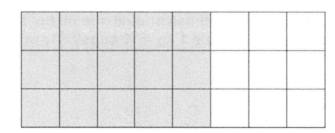

A $\frac{3}{5}$

C $\frac{3}{8}$

B $\frac{2}{5}$

D $\frac{5}{8}$

Common Core Standard 5.NF.3 – Number & Operations – Fractions

☐ **Janice, Marsha, Becky, JaeLyn, and Audrey want to divide 51 teddy bears equally. How many teddy bears will each girl receive? What two whole numbers would the correct answer lie between? Be sure to show your work.**

A $10\frac{1}{5}$; 9 and 10

C $12\frac{3}{4}$; 12 and 13

B $10\frac{1}{5}$; 10 and 11

D $8\frac{1}{2}$; 8 and 9

Common Core Standard 5.NF.3 – Number & Operations – Fractions

☐ **What fraction best describes the shaded model below?**

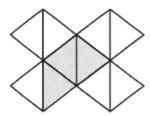

A $\frac{3}{8}$

C $\frac{3}{10}$

B $\frac{1}{3}$

D $\frac{7}{10}$

Common Core Standard 5.NF.3 – Number & Operations – Fractions

☐ **If there were 39 bones to be divided by 5 dogs equally, how many bones would each dog receive? What two whole numbers would the correct answer lie between? Be sure to show your work.**

A $7\frac{4}{5}$; 7 and 8   C $7\frac{4}{5}$; 6 and 7

B $9\frac{3}{4}$; 8 and 10   D $6\frac{1}{2}$; 6 and 7

Common Core Standard 5.NF.3 – Number & Operations – Fractions

☐ **What fraction best describes the shaded model below?**

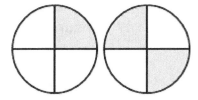

A $\frac{1}{4}$ C $\frac{5}{8}$

B $\frac{1}{2}$ D $\frac{3}{8}$

Common Core Standard 5.NF.3 – Number & Operations – Fractions

☐ **What fraction best describes the shaded model below?**

A $\frac{3}{4}$ C $\frac{4}{7}$

B $\frac{3}{7}$ D $\frac{1}{2}$

Common Core Standard 5.NF.3 – Number & Operations – Fractions

What fraction best describes the shaded model below?

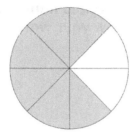

A $\dfrac{3}{4}$ C $\dfrac{2}{3}$

B $\dfrac{1}{3}$ D $\dfrac{1}{4}$

Common Core Standard 5.NF.3 – Number & Operations – Fractions

If there are 74 boxes of apples that were to be divided equally into 8 groups, how many boxes are in each group? What two whole numbers would the correct answer lie between? Be sure to show your work.

A $9\dfrac{1}{4}$; 8 and 9   C $9\dfrac{1}{4}$; 9 and 10

B $8\dfrac{1}{5}$; 8 and 9   D $10\dfrac{3}{5}$; 10 and 11

Common Core Standard 5.NF.3 – Number & Operations – Fractions

What fraction best describes the shaded model below?

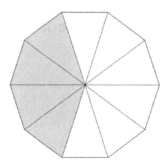

A $\dfrac{3}{4}$ C $\dfrac{1}{3}$

B $\dfrac{3}{7}$ D $\dfrac{2}{5}$

Name _____

Common Core Standard 5.NF.4 – Number & Operations - Fractions

☐ **Solve the fraction below. Be sure to show your work.**

$$10 \times \frac{3}{2} =$$

Common Core Standard 5.NF.4 – Number & Operations – Fractions

☐ **Find the area of the rectangle below. Be sure to show your work.**

$\frac{7}{5}$

$\frac{8}{14}$

Common Core Standard 5.NF.4 – Number & Operations - Fractions

☐ **Solve the fraction below. Be sure to show your work.**

$$2 \times 4\frac{3}{4} =$$

Common Core Standard 5.NF.4 – Number & Operations - Fractions

☐ **Find the area of the rectangle below. Be sure to show your work.**

$1\frac{4}{5}$

$4\frac{6}{8}$

Common Core Standard 5.NF.4 – Number & Operations - Fractions

☐ **Solve the fraction below. Be sure to show your work.**

$$14 \times \frac{7}{3} =$$

Common Core Standard 5.NF.4 – Number & Operations - Fractions

☐ **Find the area of the rectangle below. Be sure to show your work.**

$\frac{1}{3}$

$\frac{6}{11}$

Common Core Standard 5.NF.4 – Number & Operations - Fractions

Find the area of the rectangle below. Be sure to show your work.

$3\frac{1}{8}$

$3\frac{2}{7}$

Common Core Standard 5.NF.4 – Number & Operations - Fractions

Solve the fraction below. Be sure to show your work.

$$15 \times \frac{20}{9} =$$

Common Core Standard 5.NF.4 – Number & Operations - Fractions

Find the area of the rectangle below. Be sure to show your work.

$6\frac{1}{9}$

$7\frac{8}{10}$

Common Core Standard 5.NF.4 – Number & Operations - Fractions

☐   Solve the fraction below. Be sure to show your work.

$$2\frac{8}{12} \times 10 =$$

Common Core Standard 5.NF.4 – Number & Operations – Fractions

☐   Find the area of the rectangle below. Be sure to show your work.

$2\frac{1}{10}$

$4\frac{1}{3}$

Common Core Standard 5.NF.4 – Number & Operations - Fractions

☐   Solve the fraction below. Be sure to show your work.

$$15\frac{4}{11} \times 2\frac{7}{13} =$$

Common Core Standard 5.NF.4 – Number & Operations - Fractions

☐ **Solve the fraction below. Be sure to show your work.**

$$\frac{16}{2} \times 8 =$$

Common Core Standard 5.NF.4 – Number & Operations – Fractions

☐ **Find the area of the rectangle below. Be sure to show your work.**

$3\frac{4}{3}$

$7\frac{1}{9}$

Common Core Standard 5.NF.4 – Number & Operations - Fractions

☐ **Solve the fraction below. Be sure to show your work.**

$$4\frac{1}{2} \times 4\frac{2}{5} =$$

Common Core Standard 5.NF.4 – Number & Operations - Fractions

☐ **Find the area of the rectangle below. Be sure to show your work?**

$3\frac{7}{5}$

$5\frac{9}{13}$

Common Core Standard 5.NF.4 – Number & Operations - Fractions

☐ **Solve the fraction below. Be sure to show your work.**

$$3\frac{1}{2} \times 10\frac{4}{5} =$$

Common Core Standard 5.NF.4 – Number & Operations - Fractions

☐ **Find the area of the rectangle below. Be sure to show your work?**

$\frac{9}{13}$

$\frac{4}{6}$

Common Core Standard 5.NF.4 – Number & Operations - Fractions

☐   **Find the area of the rectangle below. Be sure to show your work?**

$3\frac{7}{10}$

$4\frac{2}{3}$

Common Core Standard 5.NF.4 – Number & Operations - Fractions

☐   **Solve the fraction below. Be sure to show your work.**

$$5 \times \frac{15}{9} =$$

Common Core Standard 5.NF.4 – Number & Operations - Fractions

☐   **Find the area of the rectangle below. Be sure to show your work?**

$9\frac{2}{17}$

$24\frac{1}{12}$

Common Core Standard 5.NF.4 – Number & Operations - Fractions

☐   **Solve the fraction below. Be sure to show your work.**

$$\frac{9}{3} \times 6 =$$

Common Core Standard 5.NF.4 – Number & Operations – Fractions

☐   **Find the area of the rectangle below. Be sure to show your work?**

$$4\frac{2}{15}$$

$$9\frac{7}{3}$$

Common Core Standard 5.NF.4 – Number & Operations - Fractions

☐   **Solve the fraction below. Be sure to show your work.**

$$30 \times \frac{14}{8} =$$

Common Core Standard 5.NF.5 – Number & Operations – Fractions

Determine the answer that best represents the problem below. Be sure to show your work.

$$7 \times \boxed{} = 8\frac{3}{4}$$

A   number less than 1

C   0

B   1

D   number greater than 1

Common Core Standard 5.NF.5 – Number & Operations – Fractions

Will the product be more, less, or equal to $8\frac{4}{8}$? Be sure to show your work.

$$3\frac{2}{7} \times 8\frac{4}{8} = \boxed{}$$

A   More

B   Less

C   Equal

D   None of the above

Common Core Standard 5.NF.5 – Number & Operations – Fractions

Determine the answer that best represents the problem below. Be sure to show your work.

$$\boxed{} \times 6\frac{2}{9} = 9\frac{1}{3}$$

A   number less than 1

C   number greater than 1

B   1

D   0

Common Core Standard 5.NF.5 – Number & Operations – Fractions

☐ **Will the product be more, less, or equal to $\frac{10}{13}$? Be sure to show your work.**

$$\frac{9}{7} \times \frac{10}{13} = \boxed{}$$

A   More

B   Less

C   Equal

D   None of the above

Common Core Standard 5.NF.5 – Number & Operations – Fractions

☐ **Determine the answer that best represents the problem below. Be sure to show your work.**

$$8 \times \boxed{} = 6\frac{1}{6}$$

A   number less than 1   C   number greater than 1

B   1   D   0

Common Core Standard 5.NF.5 – Number & Operations – Fractions

☐ **Will the product be more, less, or equal to 5? Be sure to show your work.**

$$5 \times \frac{2}{4} = \boxed{}$$

A   More

B   Less

C   Equal

D   None of the above

Common Core Standard 5.NF.5 – Number & Operations – Fractions

☐ Will the product be more, less, or equal to $\frac{3}{8}$? Be sure to show your work.

$$\frac{3}{8} \times \frac{10}{6} = \boxed{}$$

A   More

B   Less

C   Equal

D   None of the above

Common Core Standard 5.NF.5 – Number & Operations – Fractions

☐ Determine the answer that best represents the problem below. Be sure to show your work.

$$3 \times \boxed{} = 5\frac{3}{9}$$

A   number less than 1   C   number greater than 1

B   1   D   0

Common Core Standard 5.NF.5 – Number & Operations – Fractions

☐ Will the product be more, less, or equal to $\frac{38}{4}$? Be sure to show your work.

$$6\frac{2}{4} \times \frac{38}{4} = \boxed{}$$

A   More

B   Less

C   Equal

D   None of the above

Common Core Standard 5.NF.5 – Number & Operations – Fractions

☐ Will the product be more, less, or equal to $\frac{2}{6}$? Be sure to show your work.

$$\frac{2}{6} \times 5\frac{2}{9} = \boxed{}$$

A   More

B   Less

C   Equal

D   None of the above

Common Core Standard 5.NF.5 – Number & Operations – Fractions

☐ Determine the answer that best represents the problem below. Be sure to show your work.

$$3\frac{1}{8} \times \boxed{} = 2$$

A   0

B   1

C   number greater than 1

D   number less than 1

Common Core Standard 5.NF.5 – Number & Operations – Fractions

☐ Will the product be more, less, or equal to $\frac{5}{12}$? Be sure to show your work.

$$\frac{5}{12} \times 2\frac{1}{5} = \boxed{}$$

A   More

B   Less

C   Equal

D   None of the above

Name _____

☐ Common Core Standard 5.NF.5 – Number & Operations – Fractions

Will the product be more, less, or equal to $2\frac{2}{4}$? Be sure to show your work.

$$2\frac{2}{4} \times \frac{2}{4} = \boxed{}$$

A   More

B   Less

C   Equal

D   None of the above

Common Core Standard 5.NF.5 – Number & Operations – Fractions

☐ Determine the answer that best represents the problem below. Be sure to show your work.

$$\boxed{} \times 5\frac{3}{9} = 6$$

A   0   C   1

B   number greater than 1   D   number less than 1

Common Core Standard 5.NF.5 – Number & Operations – Fractions

☐ Will the product be more, less, or equal to $\frac{2}{3}$? Be sure to show your work.

$$9 \times \frac{2}{3} = \boxed{}$$

A   More

B   Less

C   Equal

D   None of the above

Common Core Standard 5.NF.5 – Number & Operations – Fractions

☐ **Will the product be more, less, or equal to $3\frac{1}{2}$? Be sure to show your work.**

$$\frac{11}{3} \text{ x } 3\frac{1}{2} = \boxed{}$$

A   More

B   Less

C   Equal

D   None of the above

Common Core Standard 5.NF.5 – Number & Operations – Fractions

☐ **Determine the answer that best represents the problem below. Be sure to show your work.**

$$\boxed{} \text{ x } 7 = 4\frac{1}{2}$$

A   number less than 1   C   1

B   number greater than 1   D   0

Common Core Standard 5.NF.5 – Number & Operations – Fractions

☐ **Will the product be more, less, or equal to $\frac{2}{9}$? Be sure to show your work.**

$$\frac{5}{6} \text{ x } \frac{2}{9} = \boxed{}$$

A   More

B   Less

C   Equal

D   None of the above

Common Core Standard 5.NF.5 – Number & Operations – Fractions

☐   Determine the answer that best represents the problem below. Be sure to show your work.

$$9 \times \boxed{} = 4\frac{6}{7}$$

A   number less than 1   C   1

B   number greater than 1   D   0

Common Core Standard 5.NF.5 – Number & Operations – Fractions

☐   Will the product be more, less, or equal to $1\frac{5}{6}$? Be sure to show your work.

$$1\frac{5}{6} \times 1\frac{5}{8} = \boxed{}$$

A   More

B   Less

C   Equal

D   None of the above

Common Core Standard 5.NF.5 – Number & Operations – Fractions

☐   Determine the answer that best represents the problem below. Be sure to show your work.

$$\boxed{} \times 4\frac{2}{3} = 2$$

A   1   C   number greater than 1

B   number less than 1   D   0

Name _____

ASSESSMENT

Common Core Standard 5.NF.5 – Number & Operations – Fractions

☐ **Will the product be more, less, or equal to 8? Be sure to show your work.**

$$8 \times \frac{1}{3} = \boxed{}$$

A   More

B   Less

C   Equal

D   None of the above

Common Core Standard 5.NF.5 – Number & Operations – Fractions

☐ **Determine the answer that best represents the problem below. Be sure to show your work.**

$$2 \times \boxed{} = 9\frac{4}{5}$$

A   1   C   number less than 1

B   number greater than 1   D   0

Common Core Standard 5.NF.5 – Number & Operations – Fractions

☐ **Will the product be more, less, or equal to $\frac{6}{10}$? Be sure to show your work.**

$$\frac{6}{10} \times \frac{7}{8} = \boxed{}$$

A   More

B   Less

C   Equal

D   None of the above

Common Core Standard 5.NF.6 – Number & Operations – Fractions

☐ A local shoe company is making basketball and football shoes. They made 35 football shoes in a day. If they made 6/7 as many basketball shoes as football shoes, how many basketball shoes did they make that day? Be sure to show your work.

A   35 6/7

B   30

C   31

D   20

Common Core Standard 5.NF.6 – Number & Operations – Fractions

☐ Jerold's father wanted to make lemonade for July 4th. His recipe called for 3 5/7 cups of water per container of lemonade. If Jerold's father wanted to make 2 containers, how much water would he need? Be sure to show your work.

A   7 3/7

B   6 3/7

C   5 5/7

D   14

Common Core Standard 5.NF.6 – Number & Operations – Fractions

☐ Mickael lives 4 miles from school. If he rode his bike $\frac{2}{7}$ of the distance and then walked the rest, how far did he ride his bike? Be sure to show your work.

A   4 2/7

B   2 1/7

C   1 2/7

D   1 1/7

Common Core Standard 5.NF.6 – Number & Operations – Fractions

☐ Samatha bought cupcakes for her class to celebrate Cinco de Mayo. $\frac{5}{7}$ of the cupcakes were chocolate, and of the chocolate cupcakes $\frac{1}{5}$ of them had sprinkles. What is the fraction of cupcakes that was chocolate with sprinkles? Be sure to show your work.

A   6/35

B   5/35

C   4/2

D   4/35

Common Core Standard 5.NF.6 – Number & Operations – Fractions

☐ Karl helped his father stack firewood. He stacked 2 pieces of firewood on top of each one another. If each piece of firewood was $\frac{2}{3}$ of a foot tall, how tall was his pile of firewood? Be sure to show your work.

A   2 2/3

B   2 1/3

C   1 1/3

D   3 2/3

Common Core Standard 5.NF.6 – Number & Operations – Fractions

☐ A box of pencils weighed $4\frac{2}{5}$ ounces. If Mrs. Blanco took out $\frac{5}{8}$ of the pencils from the box, what is the weight of the pencils she took out? Be sure to show your work.

A   3 30/40 ounces

B   4 10/40 ounces

C   4 7/13 ounces

D   2 3/4 ounces

Common Core Standard 5.NF.6 – Number & Operations – Fractions

A basket of grapes weighs $7\frac{1}{4}$ pounds. How many pounds of grapes are there in 6 baskets? Be sure to show your work.

A   42

B   43

C   43 1/4

D   43 ½

Common Core Standard 5.NF.6 – Number & Operations · Fractions

One package of crackers weighed $3\frac{1}{2}$ ounces. If Maria has $4\frac{1}{7}$ packages of crackers, how much do all the packages weigh in total? Be sure to show your work.

A   12 7/14

B   13 7/14

C   14 1/2

D   7 2/9

Common Core Standard 5.NF.6 – Number & Operations – Fractions

Robert and his brother Dylan had to clean up their playroom. Robert picked up 4 times as many toys as Dylan. If Dylan picked up $\frac{1}{6}$ of the toys in the playroom, how much did Robert pick up? Be sure to show your work.

A   5/6 toys

B   4/6 toys

C   41/6 toys

D   1/2 toys

Common Core Standard 5.NF.6 – Number & Operations – Fractions

☐ A piece of chocolate has $4\frac{2}{7}$ grams of sugar. If Tommy were to eat $\frac{1}{2}$ of the piece, how much sugar would Tommy consume? Be sure to show your work.

A   4 3/9

B   4 2/14

C   3 2/14

D   2 2/14

Common Core Standard 5.NF.6 – Number & Operations – Fractions

☐ Margot made a bracelet for her doll that was $4\frac{5}{6}$ inches long. If she continued to make it $2\frac{2}{3}$ times longer, how long would the bracelet be in total inches? Be sure to show your work.

A   12 16/18

B   8 16/18

C   11 16/18

D   6 7/9

Common Core Standard 5.NF.6 – Number & Operations – Fractions

☐ After Chuck's birthday party there was $\frac{1}{2}$ of a pizza left over. If Chuck gave his best friend Bryson $\frac{1}{2}$ of the leftover pizza, what fraction of the pizza did Chuck give Bryson? Be sure to show your work.

A   1

B   1/2

C   2/3

D   1/4

Common Core Standard 5.NF.6 – Number & Operations – Fractions

Marisol's hamster weighs $3\frac{3}{4}$ ounces. If she bought 3 more hamsters from the pet store, how much would all the hamsters weigh? Be sure to show your work.

A   12 1/4

B   11 1/4

C   6 3/4

D   9 3/4

Common Core Standard 5.NF.6 – Number & Operations – Fractions

A lemonade pitcher can hold $\frac{1}{2}$ of a gallon of water. If you filled up 4 pitchers, how much water would there be in total? Be sure to show your work.

A   4 1/2

B   3

C   2

D   1/2

Common Core Standard 5.NF.6 · Number & Operations – Fractions

Chanise bought $\frac{2}{4}$ of a pound of apples, however $\frac{2}{3}$ of the apples were bad. Of the apples Chanise bought, how many pounds were bad? Be sure to show your work.

A   4 1/2

B   5/12

C   4/12

D   1/2

Common Core Standard 5.NF.6 – Number & Operations – Fractions

☐ Maya wants to bathe her dog. The wash tub she uses to bathe her dog weighs $3\frac{1}{8}$ pounds when full of water. If she filled the wash tub $\frac{2}{7}$ full, how much would the wash tub weigh? Be sure to show your work.

A   25/28

B   51/56

C   3 2/56

D   3 3/15

Common Core Standard 5.NF.6 – Number & Operations   Fractions

☐ A bottle of cleaning solution uses $2\frac{1}{5}$ milliliters of lemon juice. If you wanted to make $2\frac{1}{4}$ bottles of cleaning solution, how many milliliters of lemon juice would you need? Be sure to show your work.

A   4 19/20

B   4 2/9

C   2/9

D   4 2/20

Common Core Standard 5.NF.6 – Number & Operations – Fractions

☐ Xavier made Christmas cookies. $\frac{1}{4}$ of the Christmas cookies were chocolate. Of the chocolate he used, $\frac{7}{8}$ was white chocolate. What fraction of the cookie were white chocolate? Be sure to show your work.

A   8/32

B   8/12

C   7/32

D   1/2

Name _____

Common Core Standard 5.NF.6 – Number & Operations – Fractions

☐ A pig farmer gives his pigs $\frac{5}{9}$ of a bag of barley a month. If he has 4 pigs, how many bags of barley does he give them each month? Be sure to show your work.

A   4 2/9

B   3 5/9

C   4 5/9

D   2 2/9

Common Core Standard 5.NF.6 – Number & Operations – Fractions

☐ Subbu's mother needed to wash clothes. His mother's washing machine uses $3\frac{3}{4}$ gallons of water per full load to clean the clothes. If Subbu's mother washed $4\frac{1}{5}$ loads of clothes, how many gallons of water did she use? Be sure to show your work.

A   4 2/20

B   4 2/9

C   15 3/4

D   4 2/20

Common Core Standard 5.NF.6 – Number & Operations – Fractions

☐ Chris has $\frac{3}{4}$ liters of fruit drinks in each of 8 bottles. How many fruit drinks does he have in total? Be sure to show your work.

A   6

B   6 1/4

C   6 1/2

D   6 3/4

Name _____

Common Core Standard 5.NF.6 – Number & Operations – Fractions

☐ Jonathan bought 4 pizzas for his sleepover. Each pizza weighs $\frac{7}{8}$ of a pound. How much do all pizzas weigh together? Be sure to show your work.

A   3 1/2

B   1 7/8

C   2 1/8

D   2 1/4

Common Core Standard 5.NF.6 – Number   Operations – Fractions

☐ There are 6 baskets with $\frac{4}{5}$ of a kilogram of strawberries. How much strawberries do all baskets contain? Be sure to show your work.

A   4 3/5

B   4 4/5

C   5

D   5 1/5

Common Core Standard 5.NF.6 – Number & Operations – Fractions

☐ Each of 10 students were tasked with providing $\frac{2}{6}$ of a pound of ice cream for a class party. How many pounds of ice cream will the students bring together? Be sure to show your work.

A   2 2/3

B   2 5/6

C   3 1/6

D   3 1/3

Common Core Standard 5.NF.7 – Number & Operations – Fractions

☐ **Shane had 7 large oranges. How many cups of orange juice could he make if each cup used one-fifth of an orange? Be sure to show your work.**

A   1 1/5 of a cup

B   35 cups

C   7 1/5 of a cup

D   7/5 of a cup

Common Core Standard5.NF.7 – Number & Operations – Fractions

☐ **Nemo bought a giant cookie that weighed one-sixth of a pound. He gave the giant cookie equally to 3 of his friends. What is the weight of each cookie his friends received? Be sure to show your work.**

A   1/18 of a pound

B   1/2 of a pound

C   3 1/6 of a pound

D   3 1/18 of a pound

Common Core Standard 5.NF.7 – Number & Operations – Fractions

☐ **Sawyer's mother bought one–fifth of a pound of hamburger meat from the grocery store. She made 4 hamburgers from the meat she bought. How many pounds were each of the 4 hamburgers? Be sure to show your work.**

A   1/5 of a pound

B   4 1/5 of a pound

C   1/20 of a pound

D   4/5 of a pound

Common Core Standard 5.NF.7 – Number & Operations – Fractions

☐ Charlotte and her friend made one-quarter of a liter of fruit punch juice. If they divide it equally between five glasses, how many liters of fruit punch juice were put in each glass? Be sure to show your work.

A   5 1/4 of a liter

B   5/4 of a liter

C   4 8/4 of a liter

D   1/20 of a liter

Common Core Standard 5.NF.7 – Number & Operations – Fractions

☐ Paul had one-third of a pound of playdough. He equally gave his two friends the playdough. How much playdough did each of his friends receive? Be sure to show your work.

A   2/3 of a pound

B   1/3 of a pound

C   2 1/3 of a pound

D   1/6 of a pound

Common Core Standard 5.NF.7 – Number & Operations – Fractions

☐ Jessica has one-third of a pound of ice cream. If she shared all the ice cream with her five friends, how much ice cream did each of them receive? Be sure to show your work.

A   1/18 of a pound

B   5 1/3 of a pound

C   5/3 of a pound

D   2/8 of a pound

Common Core Standard 5.NF.7 – Number & Operations – Fractions

☐ Jennifer had to write seven pages for her book report. How many hours would it take her to write the book report if she wrote one-sixth of a page per hour? Be sure to show your work.

A 7 1/6 of a hour

B 42 hours

C 7/6 of a hour

D 36 hours

Common Core Standard 5.NF.7 – Number & Operations – Fractions

☐ If a dump truck delivers one-eigth of a ton of cement and a new shopping center needed 3 tons of cement poured, how many trips would the dump truck make to deliver all the cement? Be sure to show your work.

A 32 trips

B 3 1/8 trips

C 24 trips

D 3/8 trips

Common Core Standard 5.NF.7 – Number & Operations – Fractions

☐ Sunrise Bakery used one-fifth of a bag of almonds to make 6 batches of almond cookies. How much of the bags of almonds did they use for each batch? Be sure to show your work.

A 1/30 of a bag

B 6 1/5 of a bag

C 2/11 of a bag

D 6/5 of a bag

Name _____

Common Core Standard 5.NF.7 – Number & Operations – Fractions

☐ **Mrs. Fitzhugh wanted to make a cake for her class. She used one-half of a bag of flour for the cake. If she has 4 students in her class, how much flour did each student receive equally? Be sure to show your work.**

A   8 1/2 of cake

B   4/2 of cake

C   1/8 of cake

D   2/6 of cake

Common Core Standard 5.NF.7 – Number & Operations – Fractions

☐ **Tomas went to the store and bought three cups peanuts as a snack for his lunch. If he were to pack one-fourth of a cups serving of peanuts for lunch, how many servings did he pack? Be sure to show your work.**

A   12 servings

B   3 1/4 servings

C   2/7 servings

D   3/4 servings

Common Core Standard 5.NF.7 – Number & Operations – Fractions

☐ **Suzie used one-seventh of a cup of sugar to make a pitcher of lemonade. If she were to pour the lemonade into 4 cups, how much sugar is in each cup? Be sure to show your work.**

A   2/11 of a sugar

B   4 1/7 of a bag

C   1/11 of a sugar

D   1/28 of a sugar

Common Core Standard 5.NF.7 – Number & Operations – Fractions

☐   Arin and Alex have 4 cats to feed. If they only have one-fifth of a bag of cat food and each cat received the same amount of cat food, how much food did each cat receive? Be sure to show your work.

A   4 1/5 of cat food

B   1/20 of cat food

C   1/9 of cat food

D   2/9 of cat food

Common Core Standard 5.NF.7 – Number & Operations – Fractions

☐   Julio has 4 boxes of video games. He decided to sell all the games. How many days would it take him to sell all the games if each day he sold one-fifth of a box? Be sure to show your work.

A   16 days

B   4 1/5 days

C   1/20 days

D   20 days

Common Core Standard 5.NF.7 – Number & Operations – Fractions

☐   Stephaine loves to paint. She is able to paint one-seventh of a picture every hour. If she wanted to paint 8 pictures for her family, how long would it take her to paint all the pictures? Be sure to show your work.

A   56 hours

B   8 1/7 hours

C   1/56 hours

D   48 hours

Name _____

Common Core Standard 5.NF.7 – Number & Operations – Fractions

☐ If a glass of chocolate milk is one-eigth of a gallon, how many glasses would it take to fill up a three gallon container? Be sure to show your work.

A   24 glasses

B   32 glasses

C   1/8 glasses

D   3 1/8 glasses

Common Core Standard 5.NF.7 – Number & Operations – Fractions

☐ Longville World Aquarium had six tons of fish food. How many days would it take them to use all the food if they used one-seventh of a ton each day? Be sure to show your work.

A   36 days

B   6 1/7 days

C   6/7 days

D   42 days

Common Core Standard 5.NF.7 – Number & Operations – Fractions

☐ Emily's mother bought one-sixth of a pound of potato salad. If she gave equal amounts to four people, how many pounds of potato salad did each person receive? Be sure to show your work.

A   1/10 of a pound

B   4 1/6 of a pound

C   1/24 of a pound

D   2/10 of a pound

Common Core Standard 5.NF.7 – Number & Operations – Fractions

[ ] If Marco's Pizza has six cans of tomato sauce, how many pizzas can they make with the cans of tomato sauce if each pizza uses one-ninth of a can of tomato sauce? Be sure to show your work.

A   45 pizzas

B   6/9 pizzas

C   6 1/9 pizzas

D   54 pizzas

Common Core Standard 5.NF.7 – Number & Operations – Fractions

[ ] Lusine received a box of candy for Valentine's Day. She wanted her box of candy to last six days. If the box weighs one-half of a pound, how much candy should she eat for the candy to last six days? Be sure to show your work.

A   6/2 of a pound

B   6 1/2 of a pound

C   1/12 of a pound

D   2/10 of a pound

Common Core Standard 5.NF.7 – Number & Operations – Fractions

[ ] Caleb wanted to help his older brother wash his car. The water hose they used sprays one-fourth of a gallon of water every second. If they used six gallons of water, how many seconds would it take? Be sure to show your work.

A   24 seconds

B   6 1/4 seconds

C   18 seconds

D   1/10 seconds

Common Core Standard 5.NF.7 – Number & Operations – Fractions

☐ Penelope wanted to help her local charity by collecting recycled goods. If she collected one-half of a pound of recycled goods each day, how many days will it take her to collect four pounds? Be sure to show your work.

A   1/4 of a day

B   8 days

C   4 1/2 days

D   6 days

Common Core Standard 5.NF.7 – Number & Operations – Fractions

☐ Sammie made one-fourth of a gallon of chocolate milk. He decided to give each of his four friends equal glasses of chocolate milk. How many gallons of milk did he put in each glass? Be sure to show your work.

A   1/8 of a gallon

B   4 1/4 of a gallon

C   1/16 of a gallon

D   2/8 of a gallon

Common Core Standard 5.NF.7 – Number & Operations – Fractions

☐ At the zoo there were five hippos. The zookeeper made one-eighth of a ton of food. If the zookeeper were to equally give each of the hippos food, how much would each hippo receive? Be sure to show your work.

A   1/13 of a ton of food

B   5 1/8 of a ton of food

C   5/4 of a ton of food

D   1/40 of a ton of food

Name _____

Common Core Standard 5.MD .1 – Measurement & Data

☐ Juanita made lemonade for a class party. She made 3 gallons so everyone could have at least 4 cups of lemonade. How many quarts of water did Juanita use to make 3 gallons of lemonade? Be sure to show your work.

A   12

B   7

C   6

D   1

Common Core Standard5.MD .1 – Measurement & Data

☐ The fifth grade classes made paper chains for a fall festival. Each chain they made was 5 feet 8 inches long. How many inches long was each chain? Be sure to show your work.

A   58 inches

B   13 inches

C   68 inches

D   60 inches

Common Core Standard 5.MD .1 – Measurement & Data

☐ It took Victoria 3 hours to complete her science project. Her friend Sophia finished her project in 4 hours. How many minutes did it take the girls to finish their projects? Be sure to show your work.

A   7 minutes

B   420 minutes

C   430 minutes

D   440 minutes

Common Core Standard 5.MD .1 – Measurement & Data

A new rug in Nicole's room is 4 meters long and 2 meters wide. What is the length of the rug in centimeters? Be sure to show your work.

A   4,000 cm

B   200 cm

C   800 cm

D   400 cm

Common Core Standard 5.MD .1 – Measurement & Data

The tree that Mr. Richard's class planted is 4 meters tall. What is the tree's height in kilometers? Be sure to show your work.

A   400 km

B   0.004 km

C   0.0004 km

D   40 km

Common Core Standard 5.MD .1 – Measurement & Data

Reid's puppy has a mass of 3 kilograms. What is the puppy's mass in grams? Be sure to show your work.

A   30 grams

B   0.003 grams

C   3,000 grams

D   0.03 grams

Common Core Standard 5.MD .1 – Measurement & Data

☐ Jordan's desk is 108 centimeters long. How many millimeters long is his desk? Be sure to show your work.

A   108,000 mm

B   10,800 mm

C   108 mm

D   1,080 mm

Common Core Standard 5.MD .1 – Measurement & Data

☐ What fractional part of a kilometer is a meter? Be sure to show your work.

A   1/1000

B   1/10

C   1/100

D   1/2

Common Core Standard 5.MD .1 – Measurement & Data

☐ A grocery store has limited the amount of pecans that each customer can purchase. A customer will be allowed to buy no more than 3 pounds. If Ignacio's mother bought 2 pounds, how many ounces of pecans did she buy? Be sure to show your work.

A   22 ounces

B   48 ounces

C   32 ounces

D   5 ounces

Common Core Standard 5.MD .1 – Measurement & Data

☐ A can of soda contains 354 milliliters of liquid. How many cans of soda will equal to a liter? Be sure to show your work.

A   5

B   4

C   3

D   10

Common Core Standard 5.MD .1 – Measurement & Data

☐ Christian's gas can holds 3 gallons of gas. He uses a pint of gas each time he mows the yard. How many times can he mow his yard and use one can of gas? Be sure to show your work.

A   24

B   11

C   4

D   48

Common Core Standard 5.MD .1 – Measurement & Data

☐ How many cups are equal to 2 gallons? Be sure to show your work.

A   4 cups

B   8 cups

C   64 cups

D   32 cups

Common Core Standard 5.MD .1 – Measurement & Data

☐ A football field is 100 yards long. How many inches equal to 100 yards? Be sure to show your work.

A   360 inches

B   3,600 inches

C   36,000 inches

D   1,200 inches

Common Core Standard 5.MD .1 – Measurement & Data

☐ Cordellia cut a pan of chocolate brownies into servings that measured $\frac{1}{6}$ of a foot long. How many inches long was each brownie? Be sure to show your work.

A   6 inches

B   12 inches

C   2 inches

D   3 inches

Common Core Standard 5.MD .1 – Measurement & Data

☐ A basketball game has 1 minute left on the game clock. One team used nine–sixtieth of the time left for a time out. How many seconds did the team use? Be sure to show your work.

A   69 seconds

B   51 seconds

C   9 seconds

D   960 seconds

Name _____

Common Core Standard 5.MD .1 – Measurement & Data

☐   **Ms. Sanchez made a gallon of grape drink for her gym class. She gave each student a cup containing $\frac{1}{8}$ of the gallon. How much grape drink in pints did each student receive? Be sure to show your work.**

A   8 pints

B   1 pint

C   1 gallon

D   1 quart

Common Core Standard 5.MD .1 – Measurement & Data

☐   **John bought $\frac{1}{4}$ of a pound of candy at a store for his sister. How many ounces of candy did he buy? Be sure to show your work.**

A   16 ounces

B   1 ounce

C   8 ounces

D   4 ounces

Common Core Standard 5.MD .1 – Measurement & Data

☐   **Katanna made lemonade for her friends. The recipe used 2 quarts of water. If she made $\frac{1}{2}$ of the recipe, how many cups of water did she use in making the lemonade? Be sure to show your work.**

A   8 cups

B   2 cups

C   4 cups

D   6 cups

Common Core Standard 5.MD .1 – Measurement & Data

☐ Tennis balls are packaged 3 to a box. If one tennis ball weighs 60 grams, how many milligrams would a box of 3 weigh? Be sure to show your work.

A   120,000 mg

B   180,000 mg

C   60,000 mg

D   600 mg

Common Core Standard 5.MD .1 – Measurement & Data

☐ The Williams family bought a travel trailer. If it weighs $\frac{1}{2}$ of a ton, how many pounds does the travel trailer weigh? Be sure to show your work.

A   100 lbs.

B   200 lbs.

C   500 lbs.

D   1,000 lbs.

Common Core Standard 5.MD .1 – Measurement & Data

☐ Ms. Bower bought $\frac{1}{3}$ of a yard of lace to decorate a pillow she is making. How many inches of lace did she buy? Be sure to show your work.

A   12 in.

B   4 in.

C   36 in.

D   24 in.

Name _____

Common Core Standard 5.MD .1 – Measurement & Data

☐   **Mr. Barker bought his child a wading pool. For safety reasons he put only 15 gallons of water in the pool. He used a quart jug to fill the pool. How many times did he refill the quart jug in order to fill the pool with 15 gallons of water? Be sure to show your work.**

A   80

B   60

C   30

D   19

Common Core Standard 5.MD .1 – Measurement & Data

☐   **Jonathan is 4 feet 7 inches tall. His brother is 5 feet 3 inches tall. How many inches tall is Jonathan? Be sure to show your work.**

A   11 in.

B   55 in.

C   41 in.

D   45 in.

Common Core Standard 5.MD .1 – Measurement & Data

☐   **The Byer family went on a vacation to the mountains. They hiked up one of the tallest mountains in three and a half hours. How many minutes did they hike? Be sure to show your work.**

A   200 min.

B   180 min.

C   210 min.

D   110 min.

Common Core Standard 5.MD.2 – Measurement & Data

☐ The line plot below shows the amount of juice that will be distributed to the students for the Valentine's Day party. Use the plot below to find the correct answer to the questions.

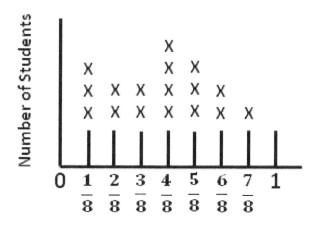

Juice in Ounces

☐ How many total ounces of juice was given at the party?

A 7 7/8   C 8 5/8

B 8 7/8   D 7 3/4

☐ What fraction of ounces did most students receive?

A 1/8   C 4/8

B 5/8   D 3/8

☐ How many students received at least ½ an ounces of juice?

A 7 students   C 14 students

B 10 students   D 12 students

Common Core Standard 5.MD.2 – Measurement & Data

☐ The line plot below shows the amount of apples by weight at the grocery store. Use the plot below to find the correct answer to the questions.

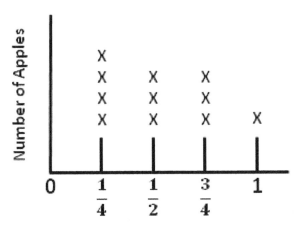

Apple Size in Ounces

☐ What is the difference between the total weight of ¼ ounce apples and the total weight of 1 ounce apples?

A ½ an ounce   C 2 ounces

B 0 ounces   D 3 ounces

☐ How many apples weighed between ½ and 1 ounces?

A 1   C 7

B 3   D 6

☐ If someone were to buy all the apples at the grocery store, approximately how many pounds would that person buy?

A 2 pounds   C ½ a pound

B 5 ¾ ounces   D 6 ¾ pounds

Common Core Standard 5.MD.2 – Measurement & Data

☐ The line plot below shows the amount of cups of water used for each cup of coffee. Use the plot below to find the correct answer to the questions.

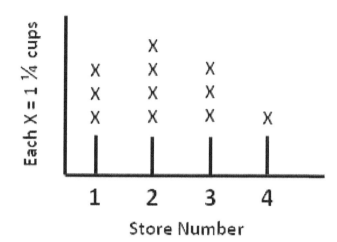

☐ Which store used the most water? What was the total number of cups of water used at that store?

A   Store 2; 3 ¾ cups

C   Store 2; 5 cups

B   Store 1; 5 cups

D   Store 1; 3 ¾ cups

☐ What was the total amount of water used at all store locations?

A   11 ¾ cups

C   13 ¼ cups

B   12 ¾ cups

D   13 ¾ cups

☐ Which store used the least amount of water? What was the total number of cups of water used at that store?

A   Store 2; 5 cups

C   Store 4; 1 cup

B   Store 4; 1 ¼cups

D   Store 3; 3 ¼ cups

Name _____

Common Core Standard 5.MD.2 – Measurement & Data

☐ The line plot below shows the number of miles each student ran last Tuesday during recess. Use the plot below to find the correct answer to the questions.

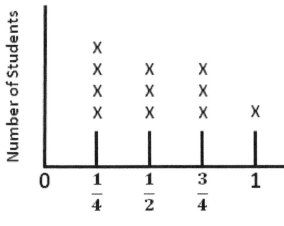

☐ How many students participated in running during recess last Tuesday?

A   7 students   C   11 students

B   12 students   D   9 students

☐ How many students ran more than half a mile?

A   7 students   C   3 students

B   4 students   D   11 students

☐ What distance did the majority of the students run?

A   half of a mile   C   three quarters of a mile

B   quarter of a mile   D   6 miles

Common Core Standard 5.MD.2 – Measurement & Data

☐ **Mr. Tomas polled his students to find out what fraction of their allowance they spend on toys. The line plot below displays the student's responses.**

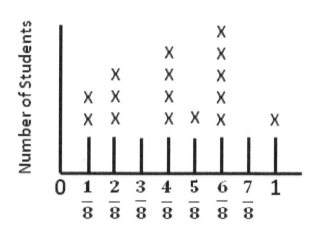

Fraction of Allowance

☐ **How many students spent at least half of their money on toys?**

A   7 students   C   11 students

B   16 students   D   9 students

☐ **What amount of the students allowance was spent the most on toys?**

A   1/2   C   1/4

B   3/4   D   7/8

☐ **How many students spent at least ¼ of their allowance on toys?**

A   14 students   C   12 students

B   16 students   D   11 students

Name _____

Common Core Standard 5.MD.2 – Measurement & Data

☐ **Mrs. Gomez is the librarian for Foster Intermediate School. She asked each of the students who had checked in a book the amount of time they spent reading their book each day. The line plot below displays the student's responses.**

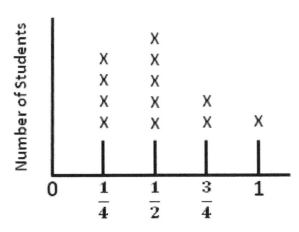

Fractions of an Hour

☐ **What is the mean (average) fraction of an hour that each student spent reading each day?**

A   3/4 of an hour   C   1/2 of an hour

B   2/3 of an hour   D   6.5 hours

☐ **How many students participated in Mrs. Gomez's survey who spent at most 3/4 of an hour reading their book?**

A   1   C   12

B   5   D   11

☐ **What was the total amount of time spent reading for those students who read for 1/2 hour?**

A   2 and 1/4 hours   C   2 and 3/4 hours

B   2 and ½ hours   D   3 and 1/2 hours

Common Core Standard 5.MD.2 – Measurement & Data

☐ Harriet measured the lengths of each student's pencil in her class and displayed the results in the line plot below.

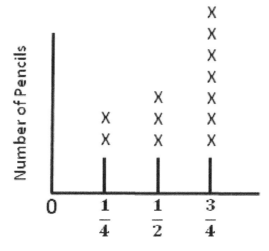

☐ If the lengths of the pencils were divided equally among the total number of pencils, what would be the approximate length of each pencil?

A   1/2 of a foot   C   2/3 of a foot

B   29/48 of a foot   D   7/10 of a foot

☐ Which pencil size do most of the students use?

A   ¼ of a foot   C   ¾ of a foot

B   ½ of a foot   D   1 foot

☐ How many students' pencils did Harriet use in her line plot?

A   12 students   C   13 students

B   10 students   D   11 students

Common Core Standard 5.MD.2 – Measurement & Data

☐ **A baseball coach wanted each of his players to try to hit 10 baseballs that were thrown to them. The line plot below shows the number of made baseballs hit for each player..**

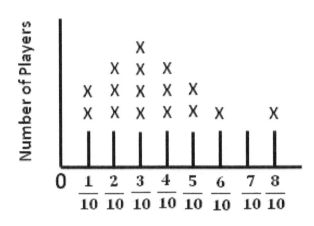

☐ **If the number of hits were divided equally among the total number of players, what would be the approximate number of baseballs hit?**

A   2/10 baseballs hit   C   5/10 baseballs hit

B   410 baseballs hit   D   7/20 baseballs hit

☐ **How many players hit a least 3 baseballs?**

A   11 players   C   8 players

B   7 players   D   12 players

☐ **What was the highest number of baseballs hit? What was the least number of baseballs hit?**

A   7 baseballs; 1 baseball   C   8 baseballs; 1 baseball

B   6 baseballs; 2 baseball   D   8 baseballs; 2 baseballs

Common Core Standard 5.MD.3 – Measurement & Data

☐ **What is the volume of the rectangular prism below?**

A   80 cubic units

B   120 cubic units

C   100 cubic units

D   110 cubic units

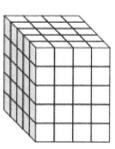

Common Core Standard 5.MD.3 – Measurement & Data

☐ **Convert the units below.   Be sure to show your work.**

200 pints = _____ gallons

A   2.5 gallons

B   25 gallons

C   30 gallons

D   2 gallons

Common Core Standard 5.MD.3 – Measurement & Data

☐ **What is the volume of the square prism below?**

A   100 cubic units

B   200 cubic units

C   120 cubic units

D   150 cubic units

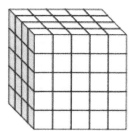

Common Core Standard 5.MD.3 – Measurement & Data

☐ Convert the units below.   Be sure to show your work.

117 quarts = _____ cups

A   480 cups

B   1000 cups

C   468 cups

D   500 cups

Common Core Standard 5.MD.3 – Measurement & Data

☐ What is the volume of the rectangular prism below?

A   50 cubic units

B   100 cubic units

C   70 cubic units

D   60 cubic units

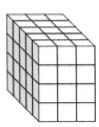

Common Core Standard 5.MD.3 – Measurement & Data

☐ Convert the units below.   Be sure to show your work.

43 ounces = _____ cups

A   5.4 cups

B   5 cups

C   4.375cups

D   5.375 cups

Name _____

Common Core Standard 5.MD.3 – Measurement & Data

☐   **What is the volume of the rectangular prism below?**

A   45 cubic units

B   36 cubic units

C   30 cubic units

D   60 cubic units

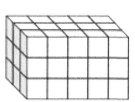

Common Core Standard 5.MD.3 – Measurement & Data

☐   **Convert the units below.   Be sure to show your work.**

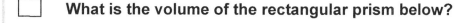

38 cups = _____ pints

A   9.5 pints

B   19 pints

C   2.375 pints

D   304 pints

Common Core Standard 5.MD.3 – Measurement & Data

☐   **What is the volume of the rectangular prism below?**

A   48 cubic units

B   60 cubic units

C   26 cubic units

D   42 cubic units

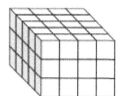

Name _____

Common Core Standard 5.MD.3 – Measurement & Data

☐   Convert the units below. Be sure to show your work.

84 pints = _____ ounces

A   10.5ounces

B   168 ounces

C   1344 ounces

D   42 ounces

Common Core Standard 5.MD.3 – Measurement & Data

☐   What is the volume of the rectangular prism below?

A   36cubic units

B   60 cubic units

C   46cubic units

D   50 cubic units

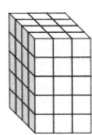

Common Core Standard 5.MD.3 – Measurement & Data

☐   Convert the units below. Be sure to show your work.

1500 ounces = _____ quarts

A   11.719 quarts

B   93.75 quarts

C   46.875 quarts

D   187.5 quarts

Name _____

Common Core Standard 5.MD.3 – Measurement & Data

☐ Convert the units below.   Be sure to show your work.

152 gallons = _____ ounces

A   608 ounces

B   19,456 ounces

C   1,216 ounces

D   2,432 ounces

Common Core Standard 5.MD.3 – Measurement & Data

☐ What is the volume of the rectangular prism below?

A   50 cubic units

B   75 cubic units

C   70 cubic units

D   65 cubic units

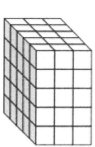

Common Core Standard 5.MD.3 – Measurement & Data

☐ Convert the units below.   Be sure to show your work.

112cups = _____ gallons

A   28gallons

B   56 gallons

C   896 gallons

D   7 gallons

Common Core Standard 5.MD.3 – Measurement & Data

☐ **What is the volume of the square prism below?**

A   60 cubic units

B   64cubic units

C   44 cubic units

D   50cubic units

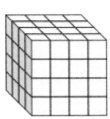

Common Core Standard 5.MD.3 – Measurement & Data

☐ **Convert the units below.   Be sure to show your work.**

240 ounces = _____ quarts

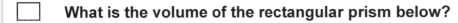

A   7.5 quarts

B   1.875 quarts

C   15 quarts

D   30 quarts

Common Core Standard 5.MD.3 – Measurement & Data

☐ **What is the volume of the rectangular prism below?**

A   20 cubic units

B   32 cubic units

C   30 cubic units

D   22 cubic units

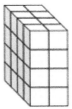

Common Core Standard 5.MD.3 – Measurement & Data

☐   Convert the units below.   Be sure to show your work.

134 pints = _____ cups

A   268 cups

B   67 cups

C   16.75 cups

D   2144 cups

Common Core Standard 5.MD.3 – Measurement & Data

☐   What is the volume of the rectangular prism below?

A   61 cubic units

B   48 cubic units

C   46 cubic units

D   80 cubic units

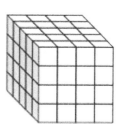

Common Core Standard 5.MD.3 – Measurement & Data

☐   Convert the units below.   Be sure to show your work.

78 cups = _____ quarts

A   4.875 quarts

B   19.5 quarts

C   39 quarts

D   624 quarts

Common Core Standard 5.MD.3 – Measurement & Data

☐ **Convert the units below. Be sure to show your work.**

260 pints = _____ quarts

A   130 quarts

B   32.5 quarts

C   2,080 quarts

D   4,160 quarts

Common Core Standard 5.MD.3 – Measurement & Data

☐ **What is the volume of the rectangular prism below?**

A   39 cubic units

B   45 cubic units

C   40 cubic units

D   50 cubic units

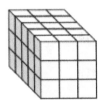

Common Core Standard 5.MD.3 – Measurement & Data

☐ **Convert the units below. Be sure to show your work.**

32 gallons = _____ ounces

A   .25 ounces

B   1 ounces

C   4 ounces

D   4,096 ounces

Name _____

DIAGNOSTIC

Common Core Standard 5.MD.4 – Measurement& Data

□ **Which figure has the *greatest* volume?**

A   B

B   D

C   C

D   A

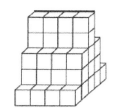

Common Core Standard 5.MD.4 – Measurement & Data

□ **A rectangular prism made of 1–inch cubes is shown below. What is the volume of this rectangular prism?**

A   10 in³

B   4 in³

C   20 in³

D   24 in³

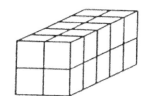

Common Core Standard5.MD.4 – Measurement & Data

□ **A rectangular prism is shown below. What is the volume of this rectangular prism?**

A   30 cubic units

B   180 cubic units

C   210 cubic units

D   48 cubic units

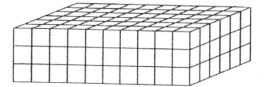

©Teachers' Treasures Publishing

Page 161

Common Core Standard 5.MD.4 – Measurement & Data

☐ **Which of these rectangular prisms has a volume of 80 cubic units?**

A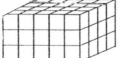

C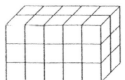

B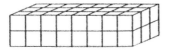

D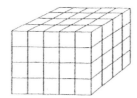

Common Core Standard 5.MD.4 – Measurement & Data

☐ **A rectangular prism is shown below. What is the volume of this rectangular prism?**

A   61 cubic units

B   36 cubic units

C   81 cubic units

D   243 cubic units

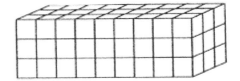

Common Core Standard 5.MD.4 – Measurement & Data

☐ **Which two of these rectangular prisms have a volume of 168 cubic units?**

A

C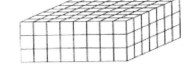

B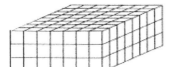

D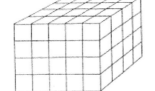

Name _____

Common Core Standard 5.MD.4 – Measurement & Data

[ ] A rectangular prism made of 1–centimeter cubes is shown below. What is the volume of this rectangular prism?

A   16 cm³

B   56 cm³

C   72 cm³

D   64 cm³

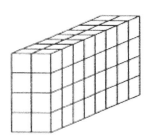

Common Core Standard 5.MD.4 – Measurement & Data

[ ] Which of these rectangular prisms has a volume of 96 cubic units?

A

C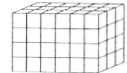

B

D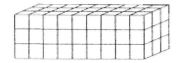

Common Core Standard 5.MD.4 – Measurement & Data

[ ] A rectangular prism made of 1–foot cubes is shown below. What is the volume of this rectangular prism?

A   33 ft³

B   54 ft³

C   44 ft³

D   30 ft³

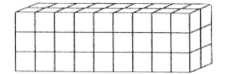

Name _____

Common Core Standard 5.MD.4 – Measurement & Data

☐ A rectangular prism is shown below. What is the volume of this rectangular prism?

A   44 cubic units

B   140 cubic units

C   56 cubic units

D   160 cubic units

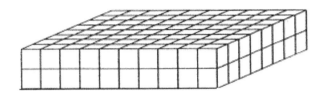

Common Core Standard 5.MD.4 – Measurement & Data

☐ Which of these rectangular prisms has a volume of 25 cubic units?

A

B

C

D

Common Core Standard 5.MD.4 – Measurement & Data

☐ A rectangular prism made of 1–foot cubes is shown below. What is the volume of this rectangular prism?

A   25 ft³

B   80 ft³

C   75 ft³

D   50 ft³

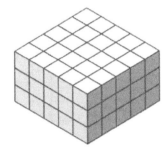

Common Core Standard 5.MD.4 – Measurement & Data

☐ **Which of these rectangular prisms has a volume of 40 cubic units?**

A

C

B

D

Common Core Standard 5.MD.4 – Measurement & Data

☐ **A square prism is shown below. What is the volume of this square prism?**

A   125 cubic units

B   100 cubic units

C   150 cubic units

D   110 cubic units

Common Core Standard 5.MD.4 – Measurement & Data

☐ **Which of these prisms has a volume of 60 cubic units?**

A

C

B

D

Name _____

Common Core Standard 5.MD.4 – Measurement & Data

☐ A square prism is shown below. What is the volume of this square prism?

A   80 cubic units

B   100 cubic units

C   20 cubic units

D   120 cubic units

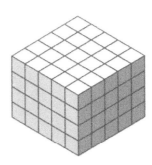

Common Core Standard 5.MD.4 – Measurement & Data

☐ Which of these rectangular prisms has a volume of 30 cubic units?

A

B

C

D

Common Core Standard 5.MD.4 – Measurement & Data

☐ A rectangular prism made of 1–meter cubes is shown below. What is the volume of this rectangular prism?

A   25 m³

B   35m³

C   80 m³

D   60 m³

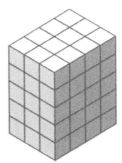

Common Core Standard 5.MD.4 – Measurement & Data

Which of these objects have a volume of 40 cubic units?

A

C

B

D

Common Core Standard 5.MD.4 – Measurement & Data

A rectangular prism is shown below. What is the volume of this rectangular prism?

A   35 cubic units

B   55 cubic units

C   45 cubic units

D   40 cubic units

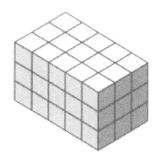

Common Core Standard 5.MD.4 – Measurement & Data

Which of these prisms has a volume of 18 cubic units?

A

C

B

D

Name _____

Common Core Standard 5.MD.4 – Measurement & Data

☐ **A rectangular prism is shown below. What is the volume of this rectangular prism?**

A   36 cubic units

B   24 cubic units

C   30 cubic units

D   48 cubic units

Common Core Standard 5.MD.4 – Measurement & Data

☐ **Which of these rectangular prisms has a volume of 36 cubic units?**

A   C

B   D

Common Core Standard 5.MD.4 – Measurement & Data

☐ **A rectangular prism made of 1–cm cubes is shown below. What is the volume of this rectangular prism?**

A   80 cm³

B   50 cm³

C   64 cm³

D   100 cm³

Common Core Standard 5.MD.5 – Measurement & Data

□   **What is the volume of the cube below? Be sure to show your work.**

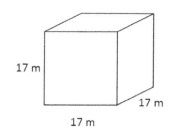

17 m

17 m

17 m

_____ cubic meters

Common Core Standard 5.MD.5 – Measurement & Data

□   **The picture below shows the rectangular prism and its dimensions. What is the *volume* of the rectangular prism?**

A   32 cubic feet

B   30 cubic feet

C   28 cubic feet

D   26 cubic feet

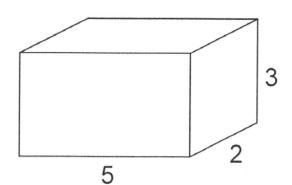

3

2

5

Common Core Standard 5.MD.5 – Measurement & Data

□   **What is the volume of the shape below? Be sure to show your work.**

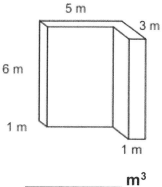

5 m

3 m

6 m

1 m

1 m

_____ m^3

Name _____

Common Core Standard 5.MD.5 – Measurement & Data

☐ **What is the volume of the shape below? Be sure to show your work.**

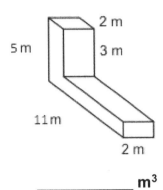

_____ m³

Common Core Standard 5.MD.5 – Measurement & Data

☐ **What is the volume of the rectangular prism below? Be sure to show your work.**

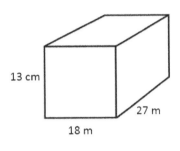

_____ m³

Common Core Standard 5.MD.5 – Measurement & Data

☐ **What is the volume of the shape below? Be sure to show your work.**

A   40 cubic feet

B   13 cubic feet

C   12 cubic feet

D   10 cubic feet

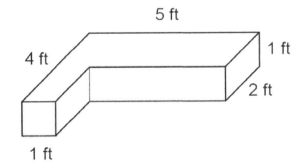

Common Core Standard 5.MD.5 – Measurement & Data

What is the volume of the shape below? Be sure to show your work.

A   312 cubic feet

B   38 cubic feet

C   224 cubic feet

D   192 cubic feet

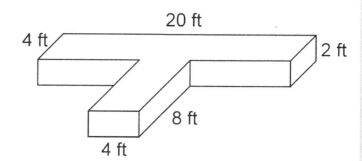

Common Core Standard 5.MD.5 – Measurement & Data

What is the volume of the rectangular prism below? Be sure to show your work.

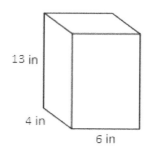

_____ in³

Common Core Standard 5.MD.5 – Measurement & Data

What is the volume of the shape below? Be sure to show your work.

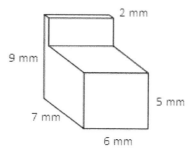

_____ mm³

Name _____

Common Core Standard 5.MD.5 – Measurement & Data

☐ **What is the volume of the shape below? Be sure to show your work.**

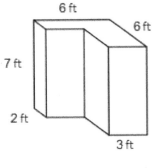

_____ ft³

Common Core Standard 5.MD.5 – Measurement & Data

☐ **What is the volume of the rectangular prism below? Be sure to show your work.**

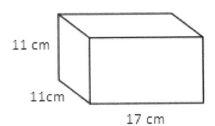

_____ cm³

Common Core Standard 5.MD.5 – Measurement & Data

☐ **What is the volume of this figure?**

A   102 cubic units

B   138 cubic units

C   118 cubic units

D   154 cubic units

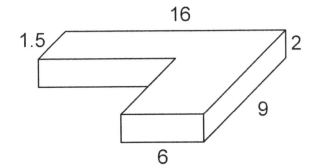

Common Core Standard 5.MD.5 – Measurement & Data

☐   The picture shows the swimming pool cover used on the city park pool. If each square is 1 square yard, and the depth of the pool is 4 yards, what is the *volume* of the pool?

A   264 cubic yards

B   128 cubic yards

C   136 cubic yards

D   260 cubic yards

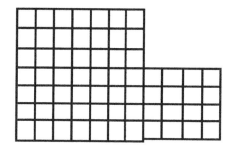

Common Core Standard 5.MD.5 – Measurement & Data

☐   What is the volume of the rectangle below? Be sure to show your work.

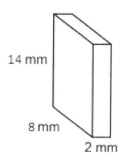

14 mm

8 mm

2 mm

_____ mm^3

Common Core Standard 5.MD.5 – Measurement & Data

☐   What is the volume of the shape below? Be sure to show your work.

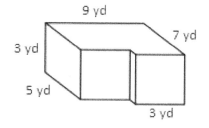

9 yd

7 yd

3 yd

5 yd

3 yd

_____ yd^3

Name _____

Common Core Standard 5.MD.5 – Measurement & Data

☐   **What is the volume of the shape below? Be sure to show your work.**

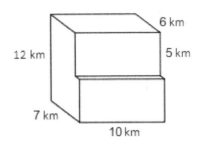

_____ km³

Common Core Standard 5.MD.5 – Measurement & Data

☐   **What is the volume of the rectangular prism below? Be sure to show your work.**

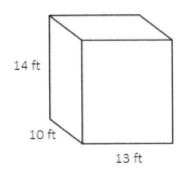

_____ ft³

Common Core Standard 5.MD.5 – Measurement & Data

☐   **This figure represents the shape of Mr. Heller's candy box. If 1 square equals 1 square inch, and the height of the box is 3 inches, what is the volume of the candy box?**

A   144 cubic inches

B   78 cubic inches

C   150 cubic inches

D   66 cubic inches

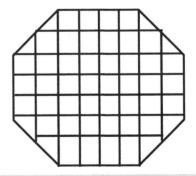

Common Core Standard 5.MD.5 – Measurement & Data

☐ Find the volume of a rectangular prism. The length of the base is 8 inches, the width is 4 inches, and the height is 5 inches.

A   40 cu in

B   160 cu in

C   20 cu in

D   17 cu in

Common Core Standard 5.MD.5 – Measurement & Data

☐ What is the volume of the rectangle below? Be sure to show your work.

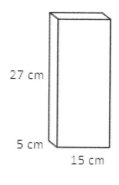

27 cm

5 cm

15 cm

_____ cm³

Common Core Standard 5.MD.5 – Measurement & Data

☐ What is the volume of the shape below? Be sure to show your work.

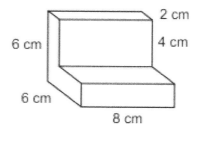

2 cm

6 cm

4 cm

6 cm

8 cm

_____ cm³

Name _____

ASSESSMENT

Common Core Standard 5.MD.5 – Measurement & Data

☐   **What is the volume of the shape below? Be sure to show your work.**

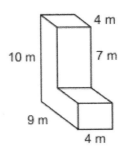

_____ m³

Common Core Standard 5.MD.5 – Measurement & Data

☐   **What is the volume of the rectangular prism below? Be sure to show your work.**

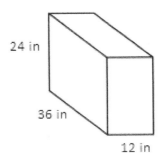

_____ in³

Common Core Standard 5.MD.5 – Measurement & Data

☐   **What is the volume of the figure?**

A   **22 cubic units**

B   **16 cubic units**

C   **32 cubic units**

D   **96 cubic units**

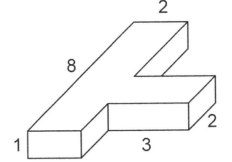

©Teachers' Treasures Publishing

Page 176

Common Core Standard 5.G.1 – Geometry

☐ **Which pair of coordinates names the location of point X?**

A   (7, 8)

B   (8, 7)

C   (7, 7)

D   (4, 4)

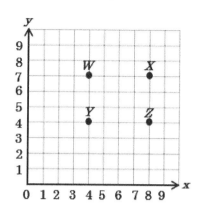

Common Core Standard 5.G.1 – Geometry

☐ **Which ordered pair appears to be below line R on the coordinate grid below?**

A   (8, 4)

B   (2, 5)

C   (5, 3)

D   (8, 2)

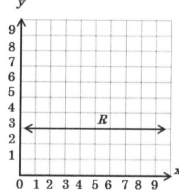

Common Core Standard 5.G.1 – Geometry

☐ **Which area is best represented by the ordered pair (5, 4) on the coordinate grid below?**

A   School

B   Library

C   Park

D   Grandpa's House

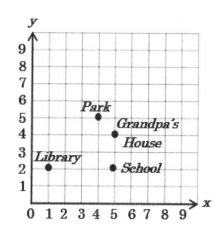

Name _____

Common Core Standard 5.G.1 – Geometry

☐ **Which ordered pair appears to be below line X on the coordinate grid below?**

A   (2, 8)

B   (6, 2)

C   (4, 6)

D   (4, 7)

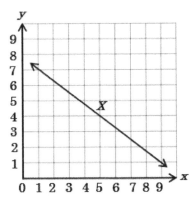

Common Core Standard 5.G.1 – Geometry

☐ **Which statement is true?**

A   Coordinates (6, 2) are located in the right triangle only.

B   Coordinates (4, 6) are located inside the right triangle and inside the rectangle.

C   Coordinates (2, 6) are located in the right triangle only.

D   Coordinates (6, 3) are located inside the right triangle and inside the rectangle.

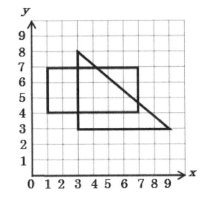

Common Core Standard 5.G.1 – Geometry

☐ **Which pair of coordinates names the location of point D on the grid below?**

A   (7, 1)

B   (1, 1)

C   (7, 7)

D   (1, 7)

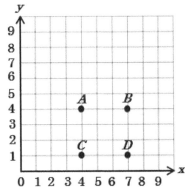

Common Core Standard 5.G.1 – Geometry

☐ Which pair of ordered numbers is inside the rectangle, but not inside the circle?

A   (2, 8)

B   (6, 4)

C   (4, 6)

D   (8, 2)

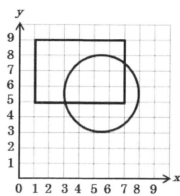

Common Core Standard 5.G.1 – Geometry

☐ The coordinate grid below shows areas in a grocery store. Which ordered pair best represents the point on the grid labeled *Paper Goods*?

A   (2, 7)

B   (3, 5)

C   (7, 7)

D   (7, 2)

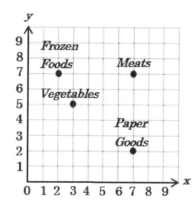

Common Core Standard 5.G.1 – Geometry

☐ Which is a true statement about the ordered pair (5, 3)?

A   Coordinates (5, 3) are located inside the unshaded and the shaded rectangle.

B   Coordinates (5, 3) are located in the shaded rectangle only.

C   Coordinates (5, 3) are located in the unshaded rectangle only.

D   Coordinates (5, 3) are not located in the shaded or the unshaded rectangle.

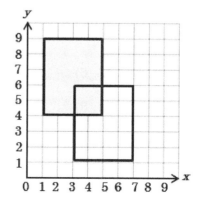

Name _____

PRACTICE

Common Core Standard 5.G.1 – Geometry

 The letters on the coordinate grid below represent the location of cars parked in a parking lot. The parking lot attendant parked another car halfway between points *M* and *P*. Which ordered pair best describes the location of the newly parked car?

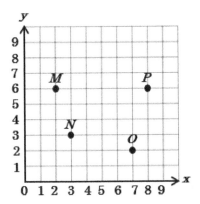

A (6, 5)

B (5, 3)

C (5, 6)

D (6, 6)

Common Core Standard 5.G.1 – Geometry

 Which pair of coordinates names the location of point *M* on the grid below?

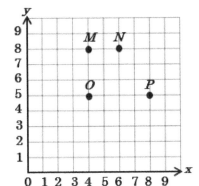

A (8, 4)

B (4, 5)

C (4, 8)

D (8, 5)

Common Core Standard 5.G.1 – Geometry

 Which ordered pair appears to be on the left side of line *B* and the right side of line *S* on the coordinate grid below?

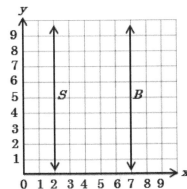

A (3, 6)

B (1, 8)

C (9, 5)

D (8, 4)

©Teachers' Treasures Publishing

Page 180

Name _____

Common Core Standard 5.G.1 – Geometry

☐ The coordinate grid shows areas of a city park. If the concession stand is located at (6, 7), which area in the park is closest to the concession stand?

A   Swimming Pool

B   Playground

C   Walking Trail

D   Picnic Area

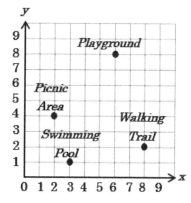

Common Core Standard 5.G.1 – Geometry

☐ Which ordered pair appears to be on the left side of line *X* and below line *Z*?

A   (3, 6)

B   (7, 3)

C   (3, 2)

D   (6, 4)

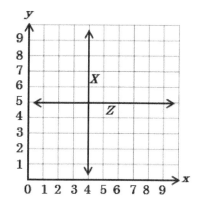

Common Core Standard 5.G.1 – Geometry

☐ Which of the following points are the same distance away from (8, 4) on the coordinate grid below?

A   Points A, C, and D

B   Points C and D

C   Points A and D

D   Points B, C, and A

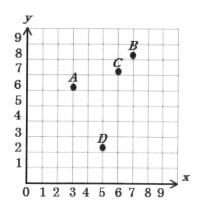

Name _____

Common Core Standard 5.G.1 – Geometry

☐   **Which letter on the graph best represents the ordered pair (2, 3)?**

A   Y

B   X

C   W

D   Z

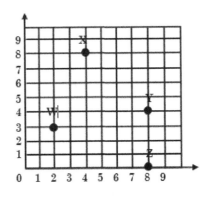

Common Core Standard 5.G.1 – Geometry

☐   **Molly and Julia were playing a game of "Hidden Treasure." Molly had hidden her treasure at the coordinates (6, 7). Which letter best represents where Molly's treasure was hidden?**

A   J

B   M

C   L

D   K

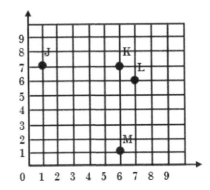

Common Core Standard 5.G.1 – Geometry

☐   **Which letter on the graph best represents the ordered pair (7, 6)?**

A   C

B   B

C   D

D   A

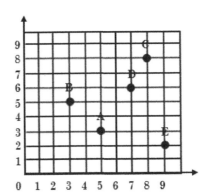

Name _____

ASSESSMENT

Common Core Standard 5.G.1 – Geometry

 Which of the following ordered pairs is represented by the letter L?

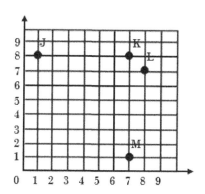

A   (1, 8)

B   (7, 8)

C   (8, 7)

D   (7, 1)

Common Core Standard 5.G.1 – Geometry

☐ If you connect all of the lines in order on the coordinate points below, which figure will you draw?

(4, 8)   (2, 4)   (6, 4)   (8, 8)

A   Square

B   Parallelogram

C   Trapezoid

D   Rectangle

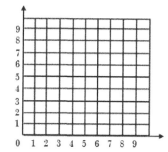

Common Core Standard 5.G.1 – Geometry

 Which letter on the graph best represents the ordered pair (8, 8)?

A   C

B   B

C   D

D   A

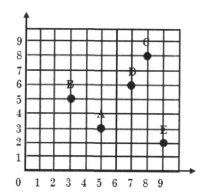

Common Core Standard 5.G.1 – Geometry

 Which pair of ordered numbers is inside the square and inside the hexagon?

A   (7, 8)

B   (5, 7)

C   (7, 1)

D   (3, 8)

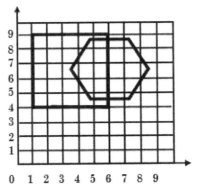

Common Core Standard 5.G.1 – Geometry

 Which letter on the graph best represents the ordered pair (3, 5)?

A   Y

B   Z

C   W

D   X

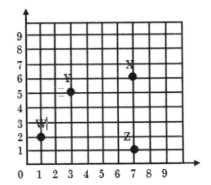

Common Core Standard 5.G.1 – Geometry

 Which letter on the graph best represents the ordered pair (9, 2)?

A   A

B   B

C   D

D   E

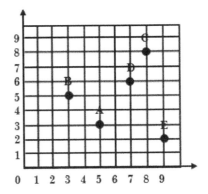

Use the coordinate graph below to answer the following questions.

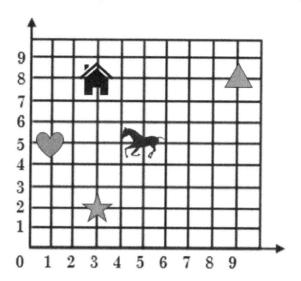

Common Core Standard 5.G.2 – Geometry

☐ Michelle's horse runs 5 blocks east (right) and then 5 blocks north (up). How far is her horse from where it started?

A   7 blocks   C   10 blocks

B   9 blocks   D   11 blocks

Common Core Standard 5.G.2 – Geometry

☐ If each line segment represents a block, how many blocks apart are Michelle's horse and the heart?

A   5 blocks   C   3 blocks

B   4 blocks   D   6 blocks

Common Core Standard 5.G.2 – Geometry

☐ Michelle rode her horse from points (5, 5) to her friends house as shown in the graph above. How many blocks did Michelle and her horse ride to her friends house?

A   3 blocks   C   6 blocks

B   4 blocks   D   5 blocks

Use the coordinate graph below to answer the following questions.

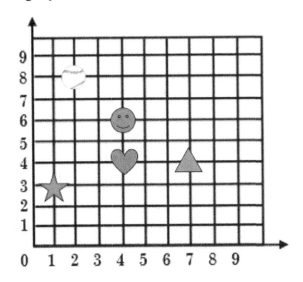

Common Core Standard 5.G.2 – Geometry

☐ **Shane went to play baseball with his friend. He walked 4 miles east (right), 8 miles north (up), and 2 miles west (left). How many miles did Shane walk from where he started?**

A   14 miles

C   12 miles

B   10 miles

D   11 miles

Common Core Standard 5.G.2 – Geometry

☐ **If each line segment represents a mile, how many miles apart are the smiley face and the heart?**

A   5 miles

C   3 miles

B   2 miles

D   1 mile

Common Core Standard 5.G.2 – Geometry

☐ **Chart how far apart the star is from the triangle if each segment represents 2 miles.**

A   7 miles

C   12 miles

B   14 miles

D   6 miles

Use the coordinate graph below to answer the following questions.

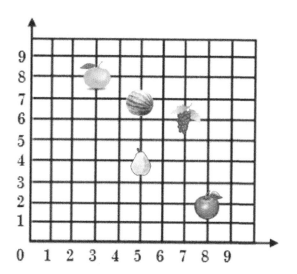

Common Core Standard 5.G.2 – Geometry

☐ Oscar loves to pick fruit from his grandmother's garden. If he were to pick grapes and each segment represents a row, how many rows did he walk to pick grapes?

A   7 rows   C   12 rows

B   13 rows   D   14 rows

Common Core Standard 5.G.2 – Geometry

☐ If each line segment represents a row, how many rows apart are the apples and the pears?

A   5 rows   C   4.5 rows

B   3 rows   D   6 rows

Common Core Standard 5.G.2 – Geometry

☐ After Oscar picked the grapes, he wanted to pick some oranges. How many rows did he walk to pick oranges after picking grapes?

A   7 rows   C   6 rows

B   5 rows   D   4 rows

Name _____

Use the coordinate graph below to answer the following questions.

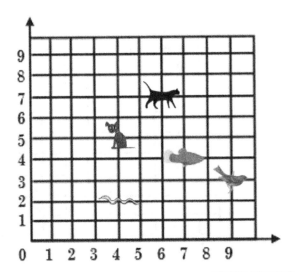

Common Core Standard 5.G.2 – Geometry

☐ Patty went to the pet store to see all the animals. If she wanted to see the puppies and each segment represents a row in the store, how many rows did she walk to see the puppies?

A   9 rows   C   10 rows

B   4 rows   D   8 rows

Common Core Standard 5.G.2 – Geometry

☐ If each line segment represents a row, how many rows apart are the fish and the birds?

A   4 rows   C   2 rows

B   3 rows   D   5 rows

Common Core Standard 5.G.2 – Geometry

☐ What are the coordinates of the snakes in the pet store?

A   (2, 4)   C   (4, 3)

B   (5, 2)   D   (4, 2)

Use the coordinate graph below to answer the following questions.

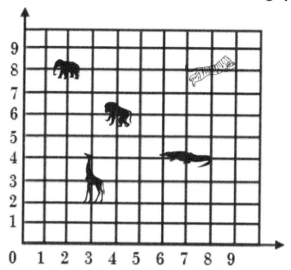

Common Core Standard 5.G.2 – Geometry

☐ Walker Elementary went on a field trip to the zoo. If the students wanted to see the tigers and each segment represents half a mile at the zoo, how many miles did the students walk to see the tigers?

A   10 miles   C   8 miles

B   11 rows   D   16 miles

Common Core Standard 5.G.2 – Geometry

☐ After the students saw the tigers, they wanted to see the alligators. How far did they walk if each segment represnets half a mile?

A   3 miles   C   2 miles

B   2.5 miles   D   4 miles

Common Core Standard 5.G.2 – Geometry

☐ If each line segment represents half a mile, how many miles apart are the giraffes and the elephants?

A   6 miles   C   3 miles

B   2.5 miles   D   5 miles

Name _____

Use the coordinate graph below to answer the following questions.

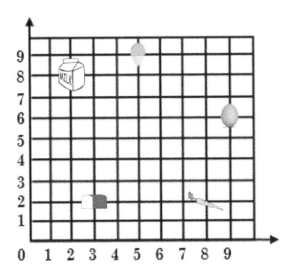

Common Core Standard 5.G.2 – Geometry

☐ Rebecca went to the grocery store with her mother. She helped her mother by getting some eggs. If each segment represents a row, how many rows did Rebecca walk to get the eggs?

A   9 rows   C   6 rows

B   10 rows   D   15 rows

Common Core Standard 5.G.2 – Geometry

☐ After she got the eggs, she needed to meet her mother at the ice cream area. How far did Rebecca walk to the ice cream area if each segment represnts a row?

A   9 rows   C   7 rows

B   6 rows   D   8 rows

Common Core Standard 5.G.2 – Geometry

☐ If each line segment represents a row, how many rows apart are the carrots and the breads?

A   6 rows   C   5 rows

B   3 rows   D   4 rows

Name _____

ASSESSMENT

Use the coordinate graph below to answer the following questions.

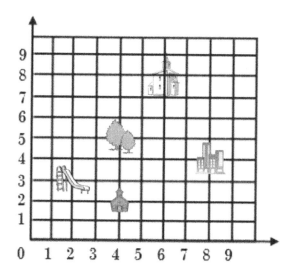

Common Core Standard 5.G.2 – Geometry

☐ Marcus went to the forest to play after he left school. If each segment represents a quarter of a mile, how many miles did Marcus ride his bicycle from the school to the forest?

A   3 miles   C   1/4 of a mile

B   3/4 of a mile   D   1 mile

Common Core Standard 5.G.2 – Geometry

☐ After he left the forest, he went to the playground. How far did Marcus ride his bicycle from the forest to the playground if each segment represents a quarter of a mile?

A   1 mile   C   4 miles

B   1/4 of a mile   D   3/4 of a mile

Common Core Standard 5.G.2 – Geometry

☐ If each line segment represents a quarter of a mile, how many miles apart is it from the school to the city?

A   1 ¼ miles   C   1 mile

B   1 ½ miles   D   2 miles

©Teachers' Treasures Publishing

Page 191

Use the coordinate graph below to answer the following questions.

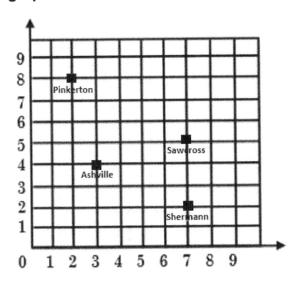

Common Core Standard 5.G.2 – Geometry

☐ Casey's Lawn Service had to travel from Ashville to Sawcross to mow yards. If each segment represents a mile, how many miles did Casey's Lawn Service drive from Ashville to Sawcross?

A   4 miles   C   3 miles

B   5 miles   D   6 miles

Common Core Standard 5.G.2 – Geometry

☐ After Casey's Lawn Service left Sawcross, they went to Pinkerton. How far did they drive from Sawcross to Pinkerton if each segment represents a mile?

A   5 miles   C   8 miles

B   7 miles   D   6 miles

Common Core Standard 5.G.2 – Geometry

☐ If each line segment represents a mile, how many miles apart are Shermann from Sawcross?

A   2 miles   C   1 mile

B   4 miles   D   3 miles

Name ____________________________

DIAGNOSTIC

Common Core Standard 5.G.3 – Geometry

☐ Which of these shapes could never have a right angle?

A Rectangle

B Right Trapezoid

C Rhombus

D Right triangle

Common Core Standard 5.G.3 – Geometry

☐ Opposite sides of parallelogram are parallel. Which of the following figures is NOT a parallelogram?

A Rhombus

B Square

C Rectangle

D Trapezoid

Common Core Standard 5.G.3 – Geometry

☐ Which of the following figures has 4 right angles?

A Right triangle

B Rhombus

C Kite

D Rectangle

DIAGNOSTIC

Name ____________________________

Common Core Standard 5.G.3 – Geometry

☐ **Parallelogram has 4 sides. Which statement is NOT true?**

A Rectangle is a parallelogram

B Parallelogram has 4 angles

C Kite is a parallelogram

D Parallelogram has 4 vertices

Common Core Standard 5.G.3 – Geometry

☐ **Which of the following figures does NOT belong to a group?**

A Kite

B Rhombus

C Hexagon

D Square

Common Core Standard 5.G.3 – Geometry

☐ **The shape below is a kite. How many sides does it have?**

A 3

B 4

C 5

D 6

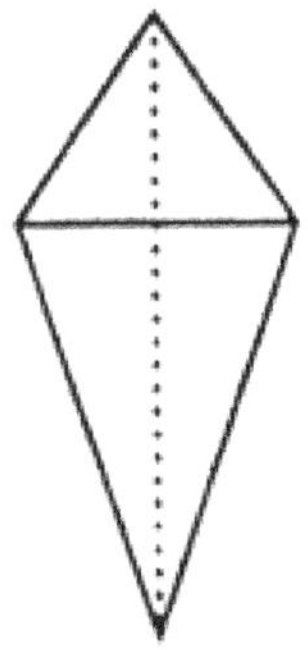

Common Core Standard 5.G.3 – Geometry

☐ Pedro was given a paper sack containing a plane geometrical figure. He could not look into the bag, but he could ask questions to determine the identity of the shape. He was able to find out that the shape had 4 sides, 2 right angles, and 1 pair of parallel sides. What was the shape in the bag?

A   Rectangle

B   Circle

C   Trapezoid

D   Kite

Common Core Standard 5.G.3 – Geometry

☐ The picture below shows the pattern for a three-dimensional figure. What figure is in the picture below?

A   Irregular decagon

B   Regular decagon

C   Rectangle

D   Triangle

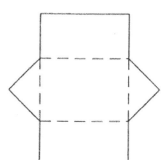

Common Core Standard 5.G.3 – Geometry

☐ Look at the drawing below. Which statement about this figure is true?

A   The figure is not a quadrilateral.

B   The figure has 3 right angles.

C   The figure has no parallel sides.

D   The figure has 2 sides that are not parallel.

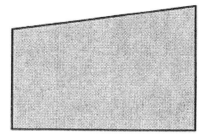

Common Core Standard 5.G.3 – Geometry

☐ **Which of these figures has no vertices?**

A   Triangle

B   Circle

C   Pentagon

D   Octagon

Common Core Standard 5.G.3 – Geometry

☐ **The figure below is a rectangular prism. Which plane figure is the side of a rectangular prism?**

A   Pentagon

B   Hexagon

C   Rectangle

D   Square

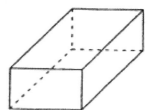

Common Core Standard 5.G.3 – Geometry

☐ **The shape below is a triangular pyramid. Which plane figure is the side of a triangular pyramid?**

A   Triangle

B   Quadrilateral

C   Hexagon

D   Octagon

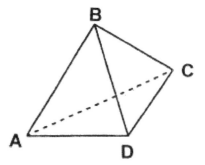

Common Core Standard 5.G.3 – Geometry

☐ Identify the true statement about the base of the figure below.

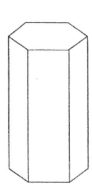

A   There are 10 sides.

B   It is a hexagon.

C   It is a circle.

D   All sides are perpendicular
         to each other.

Common Core Standard 5.G.3 – Geometry

☐ The picture below shows a three-dimensional figure. How many sides
   does its base have?

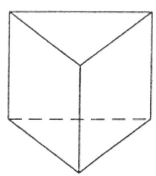

A   6

B   5

C   4

D   3

Common Core Standard 5.G.3 – Geometry

☐ How can a rectangle be described?

A   A figure with 4 sides and 4 right angles.

B   A figure with 4 sides and 4 acute angles.

C   A figure with parallel opposite sides.

D   A figure with perpendicular diagonals.

Common Core Standard 5.G.3 – Geometry

☐ **How can a regular polygon be described?**

A   It has equal sides

B   It has equal angles

C   It has equal sides and angles

D   It has an equal number of sides and angles

Common Core Standard 5.G.3 – Geometry

☐ **Look at the figure below. Which statement about the base of this figure is true?**

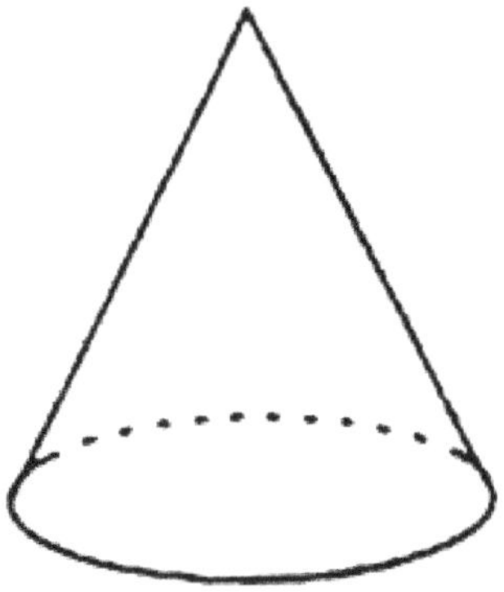

A   The base has 2 vertices.

B   The base has no vertices.

C   The base is a rectangle.

D   The base is a triangle.

Common Core Standard 5.G.3 – Geometry

☐ **Which of these shapes could have perpendicular lines?**

A   Isosceles triangle

B   Circle

C   Sphere

D   Rectangle

Name ____________________

ASSESSMENT

Common Core Standard 5.G.3 – Geometry

☐ **The figure below is a square pyramid. How many right angles does the figure have?**

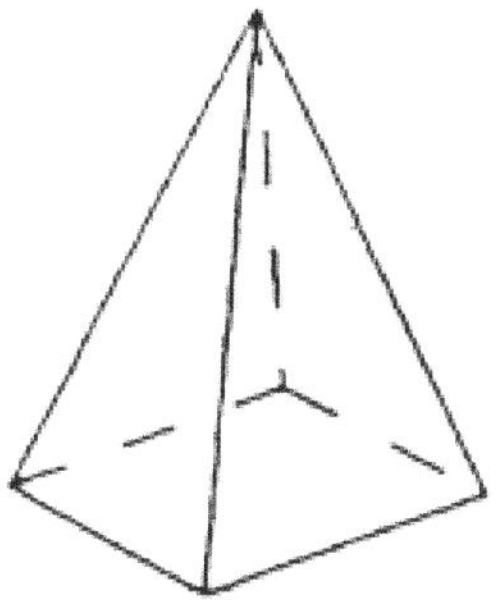

A 0

B 1

C 2

D 4

Common Core Standard 5.G.3 – Geometry

☐ **Which of the following figures has 3 sides and 1 right angle?**

A Isosceles triangle

B Right triangle

C Obtuse triangle

D None of the above

Common Core Standard 5.G.3 – Geometry

☐ **Which of the following figures has 3 sides and 2 right angles?**

A Isosceles triangle

B Right triangle

C Obtuse triangle

D None of the above

Name _____

Common Core Standard 5.G.3 – Geometry

☐ Regular polygon has equal sides and angles. Which of the following quadrilaterals is a regular polygon?

A   Rhombus

B   Rectangle

C   Square

D   Trapezoid

Common Core Standard 5.G.3 – Geometry

☐ How can a hexagon be described?

A   A shape with 4 angles.

B   A shape with 6 sides and 6 angles.

C   A shape with 8 sides and 12 angles.

D   A shape with 10 vertices.

Common Core Standard 5.G.3 – Geometry

☐ What figure can be made if the pattern is folded on the dotted lines so that side A and side B touch?

A   Diamond

B   Trapezoid

C   Parallelogram

D   Triangle

Common Core Standard 5.G.4 – Geometry

☐ **Identify the type of shape below.**

A **Rhombus**

B **Rectangle**

C **Square**

D **Trapezoid**

Common Core Standard 5.G.4 – Geometry

☐ **Identify the type of shape below.**

A **Rhombus**

B **Rectangle**

C **Square**

D **Trapezoid**

Common Core Standard 5.G.4 – Geometry

☐ **Identify the type of shape below.**

A **Parallelogram**

B **Rectangle**

C **Square**

D **Trapezoid**

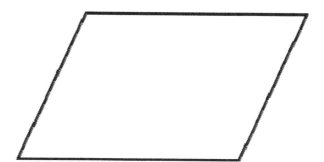

Common Core Standard 5.G.4 – Geometry

☐   **Identify the type of shape below.**

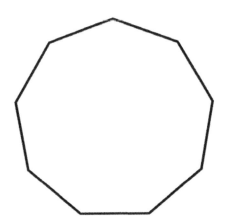

A   **Nonagon**

B   **Pentagon**

C   **Heptagon**

D   **Hexagon**

Common Core Standard 5.G.4 – Geometry

☐   **Identify the type of shape below.**

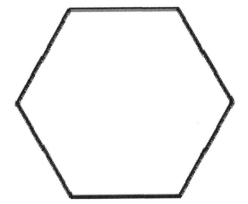

A   **Nonagon**

B   **Pentagon**

C   **Heptagon**

D   **Hexagon**

Common Core Standard 5.G.4 – Geometry

☐   **Identify the type of shape below.**

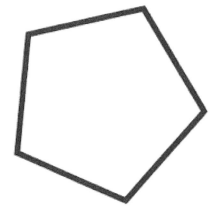

A   **Nonagon**

B   **Pentagon**

C   **Heptagon**

D   **Hexagon**

Common Core Standard 5.G.4 – Geometry

☐ **Identify the type of shape below.**

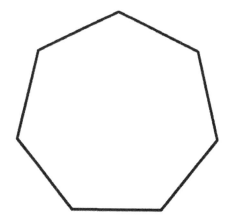

A   Octagon

B   Pentagon

C   Heptagon

D   Hexagon

Common Core Standard 5.G.4 – Geometry

☐ **Identify the type of shape below.**

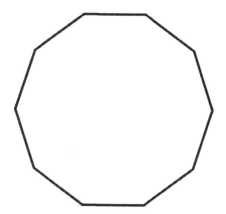

A   Octagon

B   Decagon

C   Heptagon

D   Nonagon

Common Core Standard 5.G.4 – Geometry

☐ **Identify the type of shape below.**

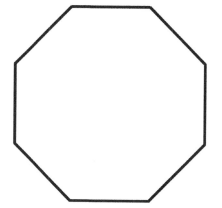

A   Nonagon

B   Decagon

C   Heptagon

D   Octagon

Name _____

Common Core Standard 5.G.4 – Geometry

☐ **Identify the type of shape below.**

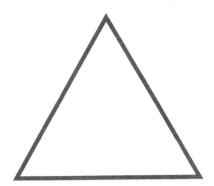

A   **Right Triangle**

B   **Pentagon**

C   **Square**

D   **Triangle**

Common Core Standard 5.G.4 – Geometry

☐ **Identify the type of shape below.**

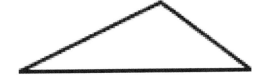

A   **Triangle**

B   **Irregular triangle**

C   **Right triangle**

D   **Nonagon**

Common Core Standard 5.G.4 – Geometry

☐ **Identify the type of shape below.**

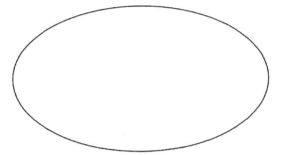

A   **Circle**

B   **Octagon**

C   **Oval**

D   **Octagon**

Common Core Standard 5.G.4 – Geometry

☐ Identify the type of shape below.

A   Irregular Octagon

B   Irregular Nonagon

C   Irregular Hexagon

D   Irregular Heptagon

Common Core Standard 5.G.4 – Geometry

☐ Identify the type of shape below.

A   Irregular Pentagon

B   Irregular Hexagon

C   Irregular Nonagon

D   Irregular Octagon

Common Core Standard 5.G.4 – Geometry

☐ Identify the type of shape below.

A   Irregular Heptagon

B   Irregular Pentagon

C   Irregular Nonagon

D   Irregular Decagon

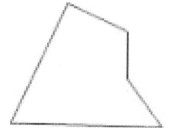

Name ______________________________

PRACTICE

Common Core Standard 5.G.4 – Geometry

☐ **Quadrilaterals have 4 sides. Which of the following figures is a quadrilateral?**

A **Triangle**

B **Hexagon**

C **Kite**

D **Octagon**

Common Core Standard 5.G.4 – Geometry

☐ **Identify the type of quadrilateral which has 4 right angles.**

A **Rhombus**

B **Kite**

C **Trapezoid**

D **Rectangle**

Common Core Standard 5.G.4 – Geometry

☐ **Which of the following quadrilaterals has no right angle?**

A **Trapezoid**

B **Rhombus**

C **Rectangle**

D **Square**

Common Core Standard 5.G.4 – Geometry

☐ **Identify the type of shape below.**

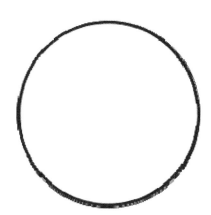

A   Cylinder

B   Circle

C   Cone

D   Square

Common Core Standard 5.G.4 – Geometry

☐ **Identify the type of shape below.**

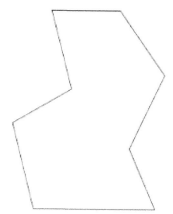

A   Irregular Square

B   Irregular Octagon

C   Irregular Pentagon

D   Irregular Triangle

Common Core Standard 5.G.4 – Geometry

☐ **Identify the type of shape below.**

A   Irregular Pentagon

B   Irregular Octagon

C   Irregular Hexagon

D   Irregular Heptagon

Common Core Standard 5.G.4 – Geometry

☐ **Identify the type of shape below.**

A   **Irregular Pentagon**

B   **Irregular Arrow**

C   **Irregular Octagon**

D   **Irregular Heptagon**

Common Core Standard 5.G.4 – Geometry

☐ **Identify the type of shape below.**

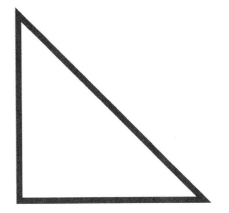

A   **Triangle**

B   **Circle**

C   **Right Triangle**

D   **Irregular Triangle**

Common Core Standard 5.G.4 – Geometry

☐ **Which of the following regular polygons has no parallel sides?**

A   **Octagon**

B   **Hexagon**

C   **Square**

D   **Pentagon**

5.OA.1

Page 1 ...... 57;236;54

Page 2 ...... 630;434;81

Page 3 ...... 7;42;252

Page 4 ...... 18;152;206

Page 5 ...... 1465;89;252

Page 6 ...... 40;16;4437

Page 7 ...... 14;206;508

Page 8 ...... 266;229;17

5.OA.2

Page 9 ...... B, A, C

Page 10 ... B, A, B

Page 11 ... C, A, A

Page 12 ... C, B, C

Page 13 ... D, B, C

Page 14 ... B, B, B

Page 15 ... A, C, C

Page 16 ... B, A, D

5.OA.3

Page 17 ... C, A, C

Page 18 ... B, B, C

Page 19 ... C, A, B

Page 20 ... C, B, C

Page 21 ... D, B, B

Page 22 ... D, A, B

Page 23 ... C, C, B

Page 24 ... A, D, C

5.NBT.1

Page 25 ... B, B, A

Page 26 ... C, C, A

Page 27 ... B, B, D

Page 28 ... D, C, A

Page 29 ... B, D, D

Page 30 ... D, C, C

Page 31 ... B, A, D

Page 32 ... B, A, B

5.NBT.2

Page 33 ... B, C, B

Page 34 ... C, B, D

Page 35 ... D, C, A

Page 36 ... C, C, D

Page 37 ... B, B, C

Page 38 ... A, C, B

Page 39 ... B, C, B

Page 40 ... A, C, C

5.NBT.3

Page 41 ... C, A, B

Page 42 ... C, C, C

Page 43 ... D, B, D

Page 44 ... A, B, C

Page 45 ... B, B, C

Page 46 ... B, C, A

Page 47 ... D, D, C

Page 48 ...B, D, C

5.NBT.4

Page 49 … C, A, A

Page 50 … C, B, D

Page 51 … B, C, D

Page 52 … C, A, D

Page 53 … A, C, B

Page 54 … D, C, C

Page 55 … A, D, C

Page 56 … C, D, B

5.NBT.5

Page 57 … 17,145,326;1,082,496;45,229,272

Page 58 … 2,473,512;6,503,661;2,445,498

Page 59 … 12,519,175;5,285,091;23,585,920

Page 60 … 3,812,985;69,785,409;5,776,416

Page 61 … 2,847,040;17,800,536;1,316,904

Page 62 … 65,086,371;1,941,118;37,037,517

Page 63 … 2,375,256;44,162,392;804,699

Page 64 … 43,307,028;3,016,328;96,920,307

5.NBT.6

Page 65 … 62; 74; 88

Page 66 … B; 86; C

Page 67 … 47; 19; D

Page 68 … 95; 83; 62

Page 69 … A; 36; C

Page 70 … 77; 62; 64

Page 71 … D; 78; B

Page 72 … 52; 25; 34

5.NBT.7

Page 73 … B, C, D

Page 74 … C, A, C

Page 75 … B, C, A

Page 76 … B, C, D

Page 77 … A, B, B

Page 78 … C, B, C

Page 79 … B, D, D

Page 80 … D, B, B

5.NF.1

Page 81 … 6 2/3;11;22 5/42

Page 82 … 1 1/6;19 32/55;79/84

Page 83 … 13/27;61 27/32;10 29/90

Page 84 … 36 17/18;14 5/6;27 12/35

Page 85 …16;3 1/63;15 11/18

Page 86 … 2 15/77;14 2/3;3 1/2

Page 87 … 6 41/42;3 29/60;11 13/24

Page 88 … 11/30;13 3/44;10 1/11

5.NF.2

Page 89 … C, D, B

Page 90 … A, C, D

Page 91 … D, A, C

Page 92 … D, B, A

Page 93 … D, B, A

Page 94 … A, D, C

Page 95 … B, A, C

Page 96 … D, A, C

5.NF.3

Page 97 ... B, C, C

Page 98 ... A, C, B

Page 99 ... D, B, C

Page 100 ... D, B, B

Page 101 ... A, B, A

Page 102 ... D, B, C

Page 103 ... A, D, B

Page 104 ... A, C, D

5.NF.4

Page 105 ... 15, 4/5, 9 1/2

Page 106 ... 8 11/20, 32 2/3, 2/11

Page 107 ... 10 15/56, 33 1/3, 47 2/3

Page 108 ... 26 2/3, 9 1/10, 39

Page 109 ... 64, 30 22/27, 19 4/5

Page 110 ... 25 3/65, 37 4/5, 6/13

Page 111 ... 17 4/15, 8 1/3, 219 7/12

Page 112 ... 18, 46 38/45, 52 1/2

5.NF.5

Page 113 ... D, A, C

Page 114 ... A, A, B

Page 115 ... A, C, A

Page 116 ... A, D, A

Page 117 ... B, B, A

Page 118 ... A, A, B

Page 119 ... A, A, B

Page 120 ... B, B, B

5.NF.6

Page 121 ... B, A, D

Page 122 ... B, C, D

Page 123 ... D, C, B

Page 124 ... D, A, D

Page 125 ... B, C, C

Page 126 ... A, A, C

Page 127 ... D, C, A

Page 128 ... A, B, D

5.NF.7

Page 129 ... B, A, C

Page 130 ... D, D, A

Page 131 ... B, C, A

Page 132 ... C, A, D

Page 133 ... B, D, A

Page 134 ... A, D, C

Page 135 ... D, C, A

Page 136 ... B, C, D

5.MD.1

Page 137 ... A, C, B

Page 138 ... D, B, C

Page 139 ... D, A, C

Page 140 ... C, A, D

Page 141 ... B, C, C

Page 142 ... B, D, C

Page 143 ... B, D, A

Page 144 ... B, B, C

5.MD.2

Page 145 … A, C, B

Page 146 … B, B, B

Page 147 … C, D, B

Page 148 … C, B, B

Page 149 … C, B, A

Page 150 … C, D, B

Page 151 … B, C, A

Page 152 … D, A, C

5.MD.3

Page 153 … C, B, A

Page 154 … C, D, D

Page 155 … A, B, B

Page 156 … C, B, C

Page 157 … B, B, D

Page 158 … B, A, B

Page 159 … A, D, B

Page 160 … A, B, D

5.MD.4

Page 161 … A, C, B

Page 162 … D, C, B and C

Page 163 … D, A, B

Page 164 … D, D, C

Page 165 … B, A, C

Page 166 … B, A, D

Page 167 … D, C, B

Page 168 … A, C, C

5.MD.5

Page 169 … 4913; B; 48

Page 170 …56; 6318; C

Page 171 … C; 312; 258

Page 172 … 168; 2057; B

Page 173 … D; 224; 153

Page 174 … 790; 1820; A

Page 175 … B; 2025; 160

Page 176 … 220; 10368; A

5.G.1

Page 177 … B, D, D

Page 178 … B, B, A

Page 179 … A, D, C

Page 180 … C, C, A

Page 181 … B, C, B

Page 182 … C, D, C

Page 183 … C, B, A

Page 184 … B, A, D

5.G.2

Page 185 … C, B, D

Page 186 … A, B, B

Page 187 … B, A, C

Page 188 … A, B, D

Page 189 … C, B, C

Page 190 … D, C, C

Page 191 … B, A, B

Page 192 … B, C, D

5.G.3

Page 193 … C, D, D

Page 194 … C, C,B

Page 195 … C, A, D

Page 196 … B, C, A

Page 197 … B, D, A

Page 198 … C, B, D

Page 199 … D, B, D

Page 200 … C, B, D

5.G.4

Page 201 … D, B, A

Page 202 … A, D, B

Page 203 … C, B, D

Page 204 … D, B, C

Page 205 … C, D, B

Page 206 … C, D, B

Page 207 … B, B, C

Page 208 … A, C, D

Made in the USA
Las Vegas, NV
31 March 2025